Caring for Our Shepherds

Caring for Our Shepherds

Understanding and Coping
with Burnout as a Pastor

THOMAS V. FREDERICK,
YVONNE THAI,
and SCOTT E. DUNBAR

Foreword by
JOSEPH SLUNAKER

CASCADE *Books* • Eugene, Oregon

CARING FOR OUR SHEPHERDS
Understanding and Coping with Burnout as a Pastor

Copyright © 2024 Thomas V. Frederick, Yvonne Thai, and Scott E. Dunbar. All rights reserved. Except for brief quotations in critical publications or reviews, no part of this book may be reproduced in any manner without prior written permission from the publisher. Write: Permissions, Wipf and Stock Publishers, 199 W. 8th Ave., Suite 3, Eugene, OR 97401.

Cascade Books
An Imprint of Wipf and Stock Publishers
199 W. 8th Ave., Suite 3
Eugene, OR 97401

www.wipfandstock.com

PAPERBACK ISBN: 978-1-6667-5775-0
HARDCOVER ISBN: 978-1-6667-5776-7
EBOOK ISBN: 978-1-6667-5777-4

Cataloguing-in-Publication data:

Names: Frederick, Thomas V., author. | Thai, Yvonne, author. | Dunbar, Scott E., 1978–, author. | Slunaker, Joe, foreword.

Title: Caring for shepherds : understanding and coping with burnout as a pastor / Thomas V. Frederick, Yvonne Thai, and Scott E. Dunbar ; foreword by Joseph Slunaker.

Description: Eugene, OR: Cascade Books, 2024. | Includes bibliographical references and index.

Identifiers: ISBN 978-1-6667-5775-0 (paperback). | ISBN 978-1-6667-5776-7 (hardcover). | ISBN 978-1-6667-5777-4 (ebook).

Subjects: LCSH: Burn out (Psychology)—Religious aspects—Christianity. | Job stress—Religious aspects—Christianity. | Clergy. | Christian leaders.

Classification: BF575 F76 2024 (print). | BF575 (epub).

VERSION NUMBER 040824

Scripture quotations are from the ESV® Bible (The Holy Bible, English Standard Version®), copyright © 2001 by Crossway, a publishing ministry of Good News Publishers. Used by permission. All rights reserved.

Dedications

Tom Frederick would like to dedicate *Caring for Our Shepherds* to two main shepherds in his life. First, the Rev. Thomas C. Frederick showed him how to shepherd his family and flock gently and diligently. Second, Pastor Jeremy Sung is an example of courage and vision as he leads our congregation into God's intended future.

Yvonne Thai would like to dedicate *Caring for Our Shepherds* to Pastor Drew, whose life and tragic passing motivated the writing of this book. She is grateful for her husband and sons for their continued support. Her work in this was possible due to their encouragement and love. Yvonne is also blessed by the friends and colleagues who have spent countless hours talking about their own experiences and providing feedback on this project. Finally, Yvonne is thankful for her coauthors and research team, Tom and Scott. Together they remain committed to serving the pastorate.

Scott Dunbar would like to thank Pastor Matt, who was integral in Scott's walk with Christ. The dedication and sacrifice of Pastor Matt, and pastors like Pastor Matt, have positively affected the lives of countless individuals. He would also like to thank his co-writers of this book, Tom Frederick and Yvonne Thai, without whom this book would not be possible. Scott's wife (Irene), sons (Matthew, Logan, and Hunter), and his parents (Judy and Jerry) all deserve his gratitude for supporting his academic and research journey.

We would also like to dedicate this book to all our shepherds. You so often are working on our behalf quietly pointing us to the Good Shepherd. We often neglect your good work. Worse, we often only complain about things we don't like. May God use this work to encourage and uplift you as you minister on our behalf.

1 Timothy 5:17–18:

> Let the elders who rule well be considered worthy of double honor, especially those who labor in preaching and teaching. For the Scripture says, "You shall not muzzle an ox when it treads out the grain," and, "The laborer deserves his wages."

1 Peter 5:1–4:

> So I exhort the elders among you, as a fellow elder and a witness of the sufferings of Christ, as well as a partaker in the glory that is going to be revealed: shepherd the flock of God that is among you, exercising oversight, not under compulsion, but willingly, as God would have you; not for shameful gain, but eagerly; not domineering over those in your charge, but being examples to the flock. And when the chief Shepherd appears, you will receive the unfading crown of glory.

Contents

Lists of Figures and Tables | ix
Foreword by Joseph Slunaker | xi

1 Introduction | 1
2 Overview of Burnout | 13
3 Emotional Labor and Burnout | 25
4 Work and Family Balance | 35
5 Pastoral Burnout | 46
6 Excursus on Christian Spirituality | 59
7 Christian Mindfulness Approaches to Managing Burnout in the Pastorate | 75
8 Christian Spiritual Practices for Managing Burnout in the Pastorate | 89
9 Developing a Plan to Manage Your Burnout | 104

References | 121
Index | 131

Figures and Tables

Figure 1. Aspects of Burnout / 16
Figure 2. Differentiation and Work and Family Balance/ 44

Table 1. Work and Family Balance Domains / 41
Table 2. Self-Assessment Burnout Questions/ 105

Foreword

I'VE SERVED IN MINISTRY for almost twenty years and have been fearfully close to burnout on at least two occasions. Honestly, it's hard for me to put that in writing. Pastors don't want to admit that they've been there because to do so is to implicitly say that we've been hurt by the church, that we have been in a situation we couldn't fix by the grit of our gifting, and that we have actually thought about quitting. Many of us are told in seminary that our pastoral call is irrevocable (though they don't often mention what happens at retirement . . . but that's neither here nor there) so to consider throwing in the towel feels like a betrayal of our ordination and to many a betrayal of Christ.

There is something about burnout, or the possibility of burnout, that is simultaneously easy to describe and also extraordinarily difficult to come to grips with. On the one hand, sometimes the demands of the pastorate can just be so difficult for so long that it feels unbearable. It stands to reason that a tree can only flex for so long under strong winds before it either breaks or falls. On the other hand, burnout seems like it should be an impossibility for the Spirit-filled shepherd of God's flock, the fearless leader who presses on no matter the cost and beckons the church to follow him in attack of the very gates of Hell! So, when burnout knocks at the door, we ask ourselves, "Am I too weak?" "Am I not faithful enough?" Or the very doubtful, "Am I a failure?" When your entire identity is wrapped up in being a pastor, these questions indicate that it is crisis time. But therein lies the rub: nearing

Foreword

pastoral burnout is indicative of an imbalanced identity. We forget that, first and foremost, we belong to Jesus Christ. We are God's children before we are pastors, before we are parents, before we are anything else. At a certain point in my ministry, to my shame, I had forgotten this. I knew it, of course, but in the hardships of serving a wounded church that lashed out and bearing the weight of unrealistic pastoral expectations, I had let it slide to the back burner. It took the powerful work of God to bring me back from the brink and remind me of my identity in Christ. This book aims to serve pastors and the church with this reminder and builds a theology and orthopraxy around this incredible truth. The key to dealing with and defeating pastoral burnout is a firmly rooted identity in Christ and disciplines that proceed from this foundation. In this book you'll find refreshing realism. The authors define pastoral burnout, go into detail about the unique challenges of pastoral ministry, and craft very pragmatic steps (with Christ at the center, no less!) to manage the tensions of the ministry. I could say that *Caring for Our Shepherds* is just a practical and insightful book, but it's more than that. As I read the manuscript, I felt that the authors had a keener insight into my experience than I've seen almost anywhere. I wish I had read this before I found myself on the doorstep of burnout.

To the readership: If you are a church member looking to care for your pastor, perhaps you see the initial signs of burnout in the leader you love—I am so thankful that you are reading this book. The fact that you care enough about the pastor God has put in your life to read this is a blessing that I cannot emphasize enough. Please read on and remind your pastor of his calling to serve Christ first and from there serve others. If you are a pastor who has never felt the nagging pangs of burnout—read with a serious heart. None of us are above the possibility. My prayer is that you take the wise steps to orient your life around Christ in such a way that you'll never experience burnout. Finally, if you are a pastor who is either near to or in the grips of burnout—it is not too late. Jesus Christ is able. Read on, soak in the wisdom, and take the exercises at the end seriously. Shepherds need to be shepherded and, as a vessel,

Foreword

we cannot continually pour without being poured into. Let this book pour into you.

Joseph Slunaker, PhD

Lead Teaching Pastor
Knott Avenue Christian Church

Associate Professor of Old Testament at
California Baptist University

1

Introduction

Introduction

How do you deal with stress? Do you exercise? Turn to food? Sleep? Pray? Tell yourself to work harder? Take a vacation? A quick search on the Internet for self-help suggestions to address these issues may leave your head spinning. While there are many tips, suggestions, and guides for how to deal with everyday stress and burnout, this book was specifically developed with pastors and clergy in mind. You see, the idea for this book was born in part out of personal tragedy as one of us lost our pastor to suicide. This event was both life changing and eye opening as national media outlets questioned how this could happen. As professors and researchers, we became committed to studying the unique stressors associated with the pastoral role. This proved to be difficult as our initial years of research (especially pre-pandemic) uncovered something alarming: that there was very little research and attention on the topic of pastoral burnout. Researchers in the field focused on burnout among doctors and nurses (with good reason); however, the plight many pastors found themselves facing was not well studied and, frankly, not well talked about even in the church.

As we journeyed deeper into the world of pastoring and worked with different organizations ministering specifically to pastors, we discovered that there was a unique need among shepherds to be cared for with practices that are nuanced for their callings or professions. This book, then, was born out of our heart's desire to serve and support pastors, clergy, and those in ministry. You will find that it differs from other books on stress and burnout as we narrow the focus to Christian spiritual practices as well as evidence based practical exercises that shepherds can rely on.

DifC in Action

DifC—Differentiation in Christ—focuses on the role of calling; and in ministry our first calling is to Christ. We find our identities through this calling to Christ, in which we live out Christ-centered values and goals. Our identity in Christ—our adoption into God's family by Christ's saving sacrifice—becomes our *primary* calling in life. Think about this for a second: Did your values change when you accepted Christ as your Lord and Savior? What changed and how are these values lived out in your daily relationships? Your non-Christian friends may have noticed something different about you. DifC is lived out in our relationships when our identities are grounded in Christian values and core beliefs. These core Christian values and beliefs are held, and relied upon, in both relationships and daily life. This leads us to our secondary callings.

Your secondary calling can be thought of as:

- Activities and social situations in which you live out your first or primary calling (calling to accept Christ as your Lord and Savior). This first call is sometimes referred to as the effectual call.
- Opportunities you have to express your God-given gifts and talents.
- A heart calling, or inner experience, that connects meaning to your obligations. Put another way, the heart call describes

Introduction

how an individual views a task as meaningful and important to complete (Frederick & Dunbar, 2019, 2022).

DifC proposes that our Christian identities and values are lived out in our second callings. God has placed you in a specific role and location to accomplish specific tasks. We are called to live out Christian values, through our identities and in our work environments. What is your second calling? Would people know that you are a Christian by how you act and perform in your work environment? Your particular station in life falls also under the category of a secondary calling. For example, you may coach your child's baseball team, participate in a book club, or volunteer at a local shelter. Are you a husband or wife, mother or father, son or daughter? Stop and think for a second—what do you consider to be stations in your current life? With these stations in your mind, are you living out Christ-centered values and goals? Now that we understand our primary calling (called to Christ) and our secondary calling (occupation and stations in life), the question remains: Are we able to maintain our core Christian values and beliefs in both callings?

This distinction between primary and secondary callings is crucial for pastors. The pastorate is viewed as a divine calling, and this often means pastors feel more pressure to perform at high levels even when they are struggling and hurting. Sometimes pastors merge their identity as a Christian (primary) with their vocation as a pastor (secondary). When this happens, all other secondary callings (parenthood, marriage, etc.) end up taking a back seat to being a pastor. This is one of the biggest causes of pastoral burnout, and DifC provides psychological resources to cope with this type of stress.

These tensions are powerful. Suppose we have a pastor, Brian,[1] who has been the pastor of First Community Church for about three years. He and his wife just had their second child, Melony. Their first child, Donald, was born three years before, right before

---

1. We will use several examples throughout the book. Some of these examples are fictitious in nature. Some are the combination of several pastors' stories. Names and identities have been changed to protect anonymity.

they were called to serve at First Community. As Christmas is fast approaching, school and church life for everyone at this small church enters warp speed. So many pageants. So many cookies to bake. So many activities to attend. So many expectations are placed on the pastor's family. Ellen, his wife, is tasked with being in charge of the children's Christmas program. Never mind that her youngest still requires her full attention much of the day, if not all, day. Finally, Christmas arrives, and this year it isn't on a Sunday. Isn't this a win for Brian and his family? They might actually spend Christmas together and enjoy a leisurely time of opening gifts. Not so fast! Christmas morning finds our family receiving an emergency phone call! One member of the congregation is desperately in need of help. How does Brian decide what to do? Does he leave his family and attend to his flock? What does it feel like to make the decision to leave? What does this pressure feel like for Brian? How does his family feel?

Now imagine you are Brian. How do you balance your sense of calling to be a father/spouse with being a pastor? We suggest that DifC provides the resources to aid pastors like Brian in negotiating the emotional pressures of shepherding his flock and being present for his family. If Brian is able to develop his core sense of self—Differentiation in Christ, as being beloved by God in Christ and adopted into the family of God—he will have the resources to make difficult decisions and cope with this unique aspect of job stress as a pastor. DifC allows Brian to express his core identity (primary calling) in his identity as a father and as a pastor (secondary calling).

Two important dimensions of Differentiation in Christ (DifC) that provide resources for coping with this type of stress focus on satisfaction and salience. Satisfaction means the value one gets from fulfilling a role. In Brian's case, he gets a sense of satisfaction from being a pastor and a father. Challenges arise for Brian if he bases his entire sense of self on his roles as father and pastor. If Brian's sense of self is tied into his identity as a pastor and father, he will experience the Christmas tension *personally*. He could feel like a failure as a pastor and father no matter what he does. However, if he bases his indentity in Christ, his sense of self is bolstered by his knowledge of being God's beloved child.

This leads us to the second dimension of DifC—salience. Salience focuses on our ability to determine which demands placed on us are most important—or salient—at a given time. Imagine the Pastor Brian scenario above. On the phone, Brian learns the emergency is that the member's pet dog is having a difficult birth, and Brian needs to be there to pray over the dog! Salience would allow Brian to discern which concern, either his pastoral care concern or his family time concern, should be met. Both these concerns are important as we are called to care for all God's creatures, even our pets. Additionally, God cares about us and what we care for, so these are legitimate pastoral concerns. Would praying over the phone meet the pastoral need? Is his physical presence at the farm required? How could Brian determine the salience of these important (and good) demands on his callings as a father and pastor? Salience based on Brian's identity (calling as a Christian first and foremost) aids him in deciding the course of action to maximize his expression of his identity as a pastor and father.

Congregation and Pastor's Family

The case of Pastor Brian highlights a central part of this book. Pastoral burnout comes from the tension between the congregation and the pastor's family due to the unique social context of being a pastor. The relationship between the congregation and a pastor's family is described best as ambiguity. There is much ambiguity between the boundaries between work and family life for the congregation and the pastor's family. This boundary ambiguity means that both the congregation and the family have difficulty determining how and when (and sometimes where) the pastor belongs. Boundary ambiguity (BA) is often expressed in expectations (realistic and unrealistic) as well as time demands ("Pastor, we would appreciate your attendance when my second cousin, twice removed, has her sixth child, who doesn't even attend our church"). Boundary ambiguity (BA) is a major cause of pastoral burnout, and it is often classified in academic literature as inter-role conflict.

Emotional Labor

The vocation of pastoring requires the use of emotional labor. This term refers to the act of expressing socially desired emotions while on the job (Hochschild, 1983, 2012). Specifically, it is the management of feelings to create a publicly observable facial and bodily display and it involves managing one's emotions in order to conform to professional display rules in order to satisfy job requirements (Shankar & Kumar, 2014). Managing one's feelings while on the job can be accomplished through surface acting or deep acting (more on this in chapter 3). Surface acting involves simulating emotions that you do not actually feel by changing your facial expression, gestures, or voice tone in order to exhibit the required emotions appropriate to that situation or moment. Deep acting, on the other hand, involves attempting to actually experience or feel the emotions you wish to display. Unlike surface acting, deep acting requires the change of your inner feelings by altering more than your outward appearance. These two strategies suggested by Hochschild (1983, 2012) are used by service workers when they cannot express their true emotion. However, the act of emotional labor, day in and day out, can have harmful effects on pastors, including stress and ultimately burnout.

Formal Definition of Burnout and Research on Pastoral Burnout

In this book we will be talking a lot about burnout (which we will cover extensively in chapter 2), but first we must introduce it as it's understood scientifically, rather than as a trendy word everyone seems to throw around. Let's start with a brief explanation. Research shows that burnout has three components: (1) exhaustion or emotional exhaustion, (2) cynicism, and (3) inefficacy (Maslach

Introduction

et al., 2001). You can recover from these components if you know there is an endpoint to whatever or whomever is the cause. Let's continue with Pastor Brian. Pastor Brian's church had a big *Invite Your Friend and Neighbor to Christmas Service* campaign. Now it's two weeks before Christmas and his church is expecting double the normal attendance. Pastor Brian's mind races as he considers how to recruit and train more volunteers, how to squeeze more seats into the sanctuary, the importance of his sermon, which worship songs to sing, how to tactfully approach giving, etc. Pastor Brian also feels added pressure, as he realizes that this may be the only time some of these attendees will come to church. While doubling his normal church attendance is a blessing, Pastor Brian feels immense stress and weight of this situation. Pastor Brian also must shop for presents and get ready for family to visit his home. Putting yourself in this situation as Pastor Brian, how would you feel? What would your days look like?

As stressful as this situation is, there is an endpoint. Pastor Brian knows that this is only a season of stress, lack of work-life balance, increased job responsibilities, and lack of resources. However, what if the heightened level of stress did not have an endpoint? What if Pastor Brian went to work under these circumstances knowing he would deal with the same issues day-in and day-out? This is where burnout kicks in. Pastor Brian will eventually find himself emotionally and physically exhausted. This could lead to cynicism, where he distances himself from the people and responsibilities causing exhaustion. Cynicism then causes him to lose some of his effectiveness as a pastor. This lack of effectiveness is referred to as inefficacy.

These three aspects—exhaustion, cynicism, and inefficacy—are used to describe the experience of being burned out. Many professions and careers describe the lived experience of burnout using these three categories. However, pastoral burnout seems to have a slightly different experience. Francis (Francis et al., 2011; Francis et al., 2017; Francis et al., 2019) notes that pastors are experiencing high levels of emotional exhaustion and depletion, yet these pastors also experience high levels of job satisfaction. To be clear, this relationship is not a common occurrence as high levels of job satisfaction are usually associated with low levels of burnout. This begs the question: Why do pastors persist in careers with high levels of emotional exhaustion when most others in similar circumstances change jobs frequently or change careers altogether?

Viewing pastoral burnout as the ratio or balance between meaningfulness in ministry and emotional exhaustion in ministry aids us in understanding how this experience impacts pastors. First, deriving a sense of the meaningfulness of ministry is tied into a sense of calling. Using DifC language, meaningful ministry provides a sense of *enduring satisfaction* based on fulfilling God's call to shepherd his flock. This satisfaction is based primarily on one's identity in Christ as a Christian (primary calling) and expressed as a pastor and father (secondary calling). This sense of satisfaction provides an emotional buffer when there are tensions in other areas of one's life—between the congregation and the pastor's family. When pastors lose their sense of the meaningfulness of ministry and have increased experiences of exhaustion, there is a high chance of burnout occurring.

One of the ways the meaningfulness of ministry becomes depleted occurs when there are conflicting roles between family and congregation. When pastors see this conflict as personally their fault, they begin to question the meaningfulness of ministry. DifC as salience aids us here. Pastors need identity-based tools to discern which priority or call takes precedence over the other. Salience allows the pastor to decide which priority or ministry demand is most important at a given time. Prioritizing one ministry demand over the other allows one to make these decisions based on one's identity in Christ. Further, satisfaction based on the various callings is shared. The pastor's sense of satisfaction is mainly based on his identity in Christ. However, being both a father and pastor contributes to this sense of satisfaction. When there is conflict in one of these roles, the pastor's satisfaction is not completely emptied, as it is not tied into a single role.

Returning to Pastor Brian, he is confident in his identity as God's child in Christ, and he's been affirmed in his calling to

Introduction

shepherd the flock. Further, he loves being a dad, despite the lack of sleep due to living with a newborn. All he wanted to do was spend a peaceful Christmas opening presents when that phone rang! The time demands challenge his satisfaction of being present with his family. If he doesn't have the resources needed internally and based on his role as a father, his satisfaction as a pastor could be challenged. After hearing the congregant's need, he needs to discern how best to meet his time demands—as a pastor and as a father. His identity in Christ allows him to experience the potential disappointments from either his family (Daddy must visit Aunt May at the farm now; her puppy is not feeling well at all) or the congregation (Pastor Brian cannot be physically present for you right now; however, Pastor can pray over the phone now with you). Salience allows Pastor Brian to make a very difficult decision in order to meet both sets of ministry demands to the best of his ability.

Additionally, emotional labor will start as soon as Pastor Brian decides to answer the phone call from his congregant. As he was in the middle of Christmas morning with his family, he is understandably irritated. However, he knows he cannot answer the phone with an angry tone. Therefore, he shakes off his very real and valid feelings over being disrupted and puts on a pleasant tone because he realizes that's what is expected of him in this situation. He is surface acting. As he listens to the other end and hears the reason behind the call, he begins to realize the seriousness of the situation and his previous feelings of annoyance become transformed to one of concern as he matches the distress of his congregant's feelings (deep acting). This experience of emotional labor will impact his decision to stay with his family or leave to attend to his sheep.

Structure of the Book

Chapter 2 of this book will describe the experience of burnout and its impact on workers. Some of the questions answered in this chapter include: What is burnout? What are the costs or burdens of burnout? Business or corporate costs (training/hiring new employees)? The physical effects of burnout? The psychological effects of burnout? What are the factors contributing to burnout (Maslach's six areas of organizational life) and organizational factors? What do we know from business and industrial and organizational psychology? Burnout will also be described as *acedia* based on a Christian worldview perspective.

Chapter 3 will describe the emerging research tying one's emotional regulation strategies with burnout. For social service providers like pastors, emotional labor strategies are used when dealing with people vocationally. That is, emotional labor describes how pastors utilize specific tools in order to respond to the people they are trying to serve. These strategies are generally grouped into (1) surface acting and (2) deep acting. Emerging research on burnout and the human services is connecting these strategies to the experience of burnout.

Chapter 4 will describe the family dimension of burnout. Burnout is seen increasingly as resulting from conflict in relationship contexts, what we called ministry demands above. Work and family balance (WFB) provides a framework for understanding this conflict. After reviewing research on WFB and burnout, attention will be given to the family contributions for coping with burnout—differentiation. Differentiation provides the background for understanding DifC and ultimately our model of salience and satisfaction.

Chapter 5 will describe Cameron Lee's (1989, 2006) research on ministry demands and boundary violations (*Life in a Glass House* metaphor) that contribute to work and family balance and the pastorate. Lee describes how the pastor's family is in a unique social context which may contribute greatly to burnout due to work and family conflict. Pastoral burnout will also be described as the ratio of the experience of exhaustion and calling and ministry satisfaction (Francis et al., 2011; Francis et al., 2017; Francis et al., 2019). One of Francis's and his colleagues' (2011; 2017; 2018; 2019) main contributions focuses on understanding how pastors tend to report high levels of burnout yet remain in ministry.

Introduction

Finally, chapter 5 will present our DifC model for coping with burnout as a pastor.

Chapter 6 is a brief review of Christian spirituality. Some of the main resources to cope with and prevent burnout are spiritual in nature. For some pastors, there is a concern over using traditional Christian spiritual practices or what are known as spiritual disciplines due the origins of these practices and their similarity to mindfulness. These spiritual disciplines are referred to generally as Christian devotion meditation (CDM). A goal of this chapter is to reclaim Christian devotional practices so that pastors may confidently use them to cope with job stress and burnout. To reconnect these traditional practices with the current church, we will utilize Richard Foster's (1998) six streams of spiritual practice. These common streams describe how ancient practices develop an intentional imitation of Christ, which is the goal of Christian spirituality.

Chapter 7 will describe some of the research on mindfulness approaches to coping with burnout. The focus here will be on identifying specific practices for pastors to use. Some of these practices are useful for in-the-moment coping strategies. Other strategies are useful long-term practices that foster deeper emotion regulation. These practices will be practical in nature and can be used in conjunction with the spiritual practices outlined in the remaining chapters.

Chapter 8 will present Christian devotional meditation (CDM) practices to cope with burnout. Three CDM practices—*lectio divina*, saying the Jesus Prayer, and centering prayer—will be offered to aid in coping with ministerial stress and to prevent burnout. CDM or what are sometimes known as Christian contemplative practices are uniquely suited to develop the emotional resources pastors need for coping with burnout. Pastors experience spiritual emptiness (what we describe as acedia in chapter 2) due to two unique aspects of pastoral life. First, since pastors often work alongside with their families in the church while simultaneously serving their congregants, they experience inter-role conflict due to the high level of boundary ambiguity between their vocational and family lives. Second, pastors need to rely on their psychological resources to provide for their church members due to the emotional labor required of their positions.

Chapter 9 asks you to develop a personal plan to cope with pastoral burnout. The three main areas associated with pastoral burnout focus on the experience of burnout, the family context of it, and the congregation contributions to it. The first step in developing this plan is to assess your current level of burnout. Next, we need to think about the sources of this burnout—conflict between the family and the congregation (time demands and expectations)—and the congregation (organizational) contributions need to be considered. By reflecting on the levels and sources of burnout, we can tailor a spiritually focused plan to address the different sources of pastoral burnout.

As a note, we hope and pray that God will use this book to help you understand the impact and causes of pastoral burnout. The reason we wrote this book is simple: In our way we wanted to find an avenue to care for our shepherds. During this process we were often reminded of the many sacrifices pastors make for their vocations. Pastors and ministry leaders devote their lives to pouring into others, but how are their cups filled when they find themselves depleted? This is the heart of this book, and we pray the practical suggestions provided here will aid in managing and coping with stressors unique to the role of pastoring.

2

Overview of Burnout

Introduction

PASTORS ARE NOT IMMUNE to burnout nor the consequences of burnout. To tackle this pressing issue, we must first understand the definition of burnout. How would you define it? What causes one to become burned out? Moreover, what causes a pastor to become burned out? Before we jump into burnout and concepts related to burnout, let's go through a brief history of research on this important topic.

Burnout, as we now understand it, became a formalized area of study in the 1970s. Burnout has gone through three distinct phases since its birth. The first phase, dubbed the exploratory phase, took place in the 1970s and the 1980s. The focus during this phase was defining and describing burnout. The second phase took place in the 1980s and the 1990s. This phase was called the empirical phase and saw researchers move beyond solely describing burnout. Researchers tested burnout in an expanded array of occupations during this time and incorporated both quantitative and qualitative methodologies in studies (Maslach et al., 2001). The final phase is the expanding phase. During this current and final phase, researchers incorporated the effects of technology on burnout and continued to apply burnout to an ever-increasing array of occupations. Technology includes emails, texts, tablets, computers, smartphones, and other applications that keep us tied to work (Dunbar et al., 2020). Have you ever felt that you were tethered to work by your phone? Or have you ever felt obligated to check or respond to an email or text during, say, a family dinner?

Burnout continues to be a popular term, and rightly so. Some concepts useful for understanding burnout and the pastorate include compassion fatigue, acedia, areas of organizational life, work-family balance, and emotional labor. We will also look at the consequences of burnout. From your experiences, what do you think happens to an individual experiencing burnout? What happens to an organization that leaves burnout unchecked? Let's get started!

Burnout

The term *burnout* has become part of normal conversations when someone feels tired, stressed out, or overcome by some aspect of his or her life. Some even use the term burnout to describe weariness or exhaustion. Do these experiences describe how you define burnout? Is burnout more than simply the experience of feeling tired or stressed out from work or other activities? Is there more to burnout than feeling tired? Does it apply to you? Researchers have defined burnout as "a prolonged response to chronic emotional and interpersonal stressors on the job, and is defined by the three dimensions of exhaustion, cynicism, and inefficacy" (Maslach et al., 2001, p. 397). The key components of this definition provide nuance for understanding the experience of burnout. *Prolonged* means frequency of occurrence over an extended period of time. We can recover from and avoid burnout when a stressful, aggravating, and exasperating day is not the everyday normal. However, when faced with such *stressful experiences* repeatedly we may be unable to recover physically and/or mentally. In other words, *prolonged* means an extended length of time in terms of the frequency of the experience—happens multiple times a day for weeks or months even, not usually a couple of days here and there. This leads to our next key component, *chronic*, which refers to something happening repeatedly over a length of time. Again, we may be able to bounce back from a single stressful event and avoid burnout. Chronic indicates that the experience is long-lasting—weeks, months, and sometimes years. When this same or similar stressful event continues repeatedly, and we are worn out both physically and mentally. *Emotions* involve our feelings and experiences while *interpersonal* simply means the interactions between multiple people. *Stressors* are anything that causes worry, uneasiness, uncertainty, apprehension, etc. What do prolonged, chronic, emotions, and stressors lead to? All these components ultimately comprise the experience of burnout. The three components or dimensions of burnout as described in the definition are exhaustion, cynicism, and inefficacy (see figure 1). *Exhaustion* refers to one feeling worn out, fatigued, and depleted of energy. *Cynicism* occurs when a person becomes detached from concern and takes on a negative attitude. Finally, *inefficacy* happens when a person feels a low level of accomplishment, low morale, and has a reduced level of productivity (Maslach et al., 1996; Maslach et al., 2001). In other words, burnout is often thought about through (1) exhaustion in terms of experiencing apathy or lethargy, i.e., emptiness, (2) cynicism or indifference towards others, especially others one is ministering to, and (3) inefficacy, one's perception that he or she is unable to make a difference at work.

Figure 1. Aspects of Burnout.

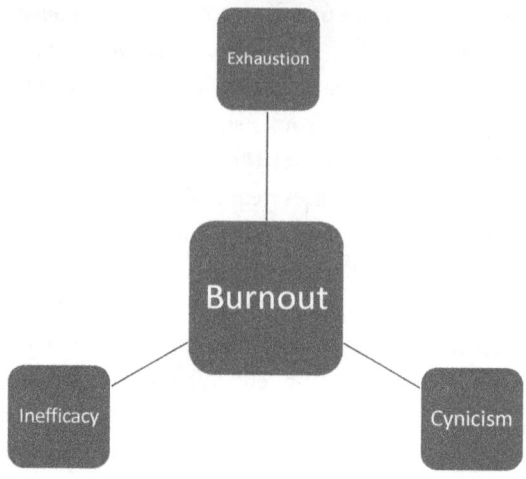

Compassion Fatigue

A similar concept that may affect pastors is *compassion fatigue*. The main difference between burnout and compassion fatigue is that burnout describes the individual experiences of those individuals directly providing services, usually social services, to others as well as those with increased likelihood of trauma (i.e., police officers, soldiers, firefighters, due to their work environment), whereas compassion fatigue focuses on psychological experiences (i.e., distress) of those individuals supporting providers that experience trauma. Compassion fatigue is usually vicarious in nature, i.e., subjective distress due to empathizing with those in occupations with increased risk for trauma. That is, counselors and other mental health providers tend to experience compassion fatigue and not burnout. Pastors unfortunately may experience both burnout and compassion fatigue. *Compassion fatigue occurs when counseling congregants, while burnout is due to ministering in non-counseling areas for the church.* In short, burnout and compassion fatigue have different causes; however, they have similar effects. When comparing burnout and compassion fatigue Udipi et al. state, "Compassion fatigue is immediate and intense and it is a deeper and more personal experience of grieving for the *tragedies that occur in patients' lives* as opposed to feelings of being overworked" (2008, p. 461, emphasis added). In other words, compassion fatigue occurs when an individual feels overwhelmed through experiencing the suffering of others and burnout occurs due to overwhelming work-related tasks or projects. Compassion fatigue and burnout may be used interchangeably or linked together. For example, individuals at risk of compassion fatigue are more likely to report being burned out, especially using the definition provided above. Individuals with a high risk of compassion fatigue may experience burnout, distressing events involving the care of others, and a large number of individuals to serve. These individuals cope with such stressful events through religion, seeking support, and blaming oneself (Udipi et al., 2008). Additionally, a pastor may experience compassion fatigue through counseling/aiding congregants through stressful events (i.e., family issues, death, loss of a job, marital strife, etc.). Such events may have been exacerbated during the pandemic as church services, Bible study groups, support groups, etc. stopped meeting or often moved to an online platform.

Acedia

Compassion fatigue and burnout describe the impact of emotional labor and drain on the self of the pastor as ministry is done in the congregation. However, the concept of burnout as used in the literature may not adequately reflect the experience of pastors (Leslie Francis and colleagues have done excellent work describing this). For example, the three main components of burnout are: emotional exhaustion, cynicism or indifference, and lack of personal accomplishment. One of the concerns with the usual definition of burnout is that pastors are often emotionally depleted and exhausted yet experience high levels of job satisfaction. Burnout is usually understood as low levels of job satisfaction and effectiveness along with high levels of emotional exhaustion and cynicism.

Pastors experiencing burnout and/or compassion fatigue may begin to question their callings. "Am I living out God's will for my life?" "Why did I treat Sister Sarah so rudely after the potluck?" "Why do I feel so drained by the congregation?" "I used to be excited to come to work and now I just feel tired and empty." Such questions describe *acedia*, which is best explained as feeling emotionally empty, having an uncaring attitude, and feeling lethargic. In other words, acedia reflects an absence of care; care is replaced by feelings of apathy, unconcern, and a lack of energy. This absence of care relates directly to the *inefficacy* component of burnout, and the lack of energy can be thought of as the *exhaustion* component of burnout. Pastors experiencing acedia, which is reflected in the experience of burnout, may lack the compassion necessary that is crucial to shepherding one's congregation. Indifference replaces this needed compassion and pastors may begin to address the needs of the congregation out of a sense of obligation. This "going through motions" voids the emotional connection and concern typically associated with the pastoral role. This lack of connection and detachment from concern directly relate to the *cynicism* component of burnout. Such feelings of apathy and indifference show that a pastor's psychological and spiritual resources are depleted, making it difficult for the pastor to compassionately shepherd the congregation. Acedia can also result in spiritual dryness and is, at worst, a lack of care and connection for God. And this disconnection from God is expressed in ministry to the congregation (see Anderson, 1997). As such, pastors may begin to question God's calling on their lives and even distance themselves from the church and/or their roles in the church (Frederick et al., 2021).

Areas of Organizational Life

We have explored how a pastor, who was once excited to serve God and others through ministry, can question God's calling due to compassion fatigue, acedia, and burnout. The questions we must then answer are: Is the person not cut out for the position? Is the organization pushing the individual past his or her threshold?

Overview of Burnout

These questions are summed up in one question, which will be addressed in the following section: Is there a mismatch or misalignment between the organization and the individual? Specifically, we will look at six key indicators of organizational life. These six key indicators aid in determining alignment between the individual and the organization. Without alignment in one or more of these six key areas, individuals may experience compassion fatigue, acedia, and burnout.

Let's start with the six key areas or indicators of organizational life: workload, control, reward, community, fairness, and values (Maslach & Leiter, 1997). These six key indicators of organizational life can create harmony when there is alignment between the organization and the employee. However, mismatches between the organization and the employee in regards to the six areas of organizational life can lead to burnout (Maslach & Leiter, 1997). It is important to understand that these six key areas of organizational life are continually changing, which means alignment or misalignment is continually changing. Let's begin with the first area of organizational life, workload.

Workload refers to the amount of job tasks/responsibilities for which a person is responsible. When the workload becomes too much for the person, a mismatch occurs between the organization's expectations and the employee's expectations. This mismatch can contribute to burnout. For example, the workload of Pastor Tim increased when his church opened a second location. He is now responsible for preaching additional sermons, managing additional staff members, leading a new congregation, etc.

The second key indicator of organizational life is *control*. Control can be thought of as the amount of perceived autonomy an employee has in performing his or her work roles. Are you able to perform your work tasks/responsibilities as you see fit, or are you told how to do your work? A lack of perceived control can cause a mismatch, which has the potential to lead to burnout. Let's look at Pastor Tim's next-in-line, Pastor Joe. Pastor Tim is mentoring Pastor Joe to take his place when Pastor Tim retires. However, Pastor Joe is feeling a lack of control as he is forced to preach sermons written by Pastor Tim. This situation can cause Pastor Joe to feel a lack of control and possibly become burned out.

The third key indicator of organizational life is *reward*. Reward can be thought of as what the employee earns or deserves for his or her work. Examples include pay, benefits, recognition, awards, promotions, etc. A mismatch between the organization and employee can occur when the employee feels he or she is not receiving the rewards he or she deserves. As one would expect, this feeling of being unrewarded for work can lead to burnout. Let's further our example of Pastor Tim (lead pastor) and Pastor Joe. Pastor Joe has been steadily taking on the roles typically relegated to Pastor Tim for several months. While Pastor Joe is taking on more responsibilities, his pay has not changed, he is not given credit in meetings, and Pastor Tim has been too busy with opening the second location to encourage, thank, or check in with Pastor Joe. In such a situation Pastor Joe may experience a mismatch and, ultimately, burnout.

Let's look at the fourth key indicator of organizational life, *community*. Community can be thought of as how well an organization responds to staff. In other words, is the culture of the organization one of positivity, respect, common purpose, mutual support, open communication, etc.? A work culture that is negative can lead to a mismatch between the employee and the organization. In our continuing example, Pastor Tim has been busy opening a second church location and Pastor Joe has been taking on many of Pastor Tim's responsibilities. Without open communication and support Pastor Joe can feel he is taken for granted or that he is not respected. This misalignment can lead to Pastor Joe feeling burned out.

The fifth key indicator of organizational life is *fairness*. Are employees of an organization treated fairly? This does not necessarily mean that all employees receive the same rewards. Again, do employees perceive that they are being treated fairly in their work environments? Employees may compare themselves to others within the organization or others in similar work roles outside the organization. Pastor Tim is in the process of opening his second location. While he sees this as an opportunity, he begins to feel that it is not fair for him to have to shoulder the responsibility of two locations. In fact, Pastor Tim spoke to another pastor whose church has multiple locations. This other pastor also told Pastor Tim that each location has a dedicated pastor. Pastor Tim may not think his current role is fair from both an internal and external perspective. This mismatch between the organization and the employee can lead to burnout.

The final key indicator of organizational life is *values*. People value different things in their work environments based upon their upbringings, family lives, cultures, ages, etc. It is up to the organization to understand what its employees work for and what its employees need. A mismatch between an organization's values and an individual's values may lead to burnout. Let's pick on Pastor Tim one more time. Pastor Tim grew up in a family where his dad was seldom around due to work responsibilities. As such, he values family time and strives to give his full attention to his family during non-work hours. However, a few church elders continue to call, email, and text Pastor Tim on his days off and late at night. This mismatch in values can lead to a mismatch and ultimately burnout.

Work-Family Balance and Emotional Labor

What role does one's family role play in burnout? Do you continually think about work responsibilities while at home? Do you continually think about home responsibilities while at work? In reflecting on your answers to such questions, let's first define work-family balance. One way researchers have defined work-family balance is "the extent to which an individual is equally engaged in—and equally satisfied with—his or her work role and family role" (Greenhaus et al., 2003, p. 513). Lack of engagement and satisfaction in either role can negatively affect the other role. Continuing with our previous example, Pastor Tim is in charge of opening a second church location. Prior to this responsibility Tim had off every Friday and Saturday. These off-days were used for family time such as having lunch with his wife and attending his kids' soccer games; completing home responsibilities such mowing the lawn, washing cars, and cooking; and resting, recuperating, and spending time with the Lord. However, he now answers phone calls, responds to emails, checks his text messages, attends meetings, etc. on Fridays as this is a typical workday for contractors and construction workers. In short, there is an imbalance between home and work responsibilities. Perhaps Pastor Tim feels stress from not attending soccer games, leaving his chores undone, and knowing that his wife is not happy with less quality time. In other words, Pastor Tim is experiencing a lack of balance in the demands between home and work.

Another important concept regarding burnout and the pastorate focuses on the *emotional labor* of work. Job demands or workload is an important dimension of organizational life. These demands are based on job expectations like projects. For service workers, there are also emotional demands. That is, service workers, like pastors, also need to respond to their customers (or congregants) in an appropriate manner. This means that these emotional responses are part of the labor involved in work. Further, the strategies employed to address the emotional demands of work are sometimes associated with increased stress and burnout.

Consequences of Burnout

What are the consequences of burnout? What is the toll of burnout in the church and for pastors? In this section we will look at the negative consequences of burnout from two main perspectives. The first perspective we will cover is the organizational perspective. Next, we will look at the consequences of burnout from the perspective of the individual. This section will be divided into two sub-sections: the physical effects of burnout and the psychological effects of burnout. It is important to note that burnout can affect the organization and the individual at the same time. Let's start with the organizational perspective.

Overview of Burnout

When considering the organizational perspective, several negative aspects of burnout are evident. The first is *turnover*. Individuals experiencing burnout will look for a different job or the same job at a different organization. This causes the organization to have to recruit, hire, and train a new person. Costs of replacing an employee range; however, a good rule of thumb is that it costs one-third to one-half of a worker's annual salary to recruit and train a new/replacement employee (Physician Practice Perspectives, 2016). The timeline and associated costs can be considerably higher when replacing a pastor due to factors such as a limited pool of applicants and specific requirements. Examples that make it difficult to recruit and hire a pastor include preaching experience and ability, exact denomination requirements, interpretation of the Bible, higher education degree, counseling abilities, leadership experiences, etc. In other words, it is often more difficult for a church to hire a pastor than it is for a company to hire a new salesperson. To mitigate this hiring debacle many churches have moved to internal succession planning (training/grooming the next pastor from within the church). However, how long will this new pastor stay if the job role, responsibilities, etc. are the same as they were for the pastor who left due to burnout?

A person may elect to stay on the job even while experiencing burnout because they need the money, lack of other job opportunities, or a sense of obligation. Organizations and churches are negatively affected by individuals who elect to stay on the job while experiencing burnout. A study by Maxon (1999) found that consequences of burnout include workplace violence, decreased customer satisfaction, inappropriate behavior, tardiness, decreased loyalty, risk of on-the-job injury, and increased employee complaints. Combining such aspects leads to a negative work culture that affects those employed by the organization or church and those who are customers or parishioners. The negative effects can cause parishioners to find a different church and it can cause church employees to leave their positions (turnover). Let's use Pastor Tim as an example. He is experiencing burnout but stays on the job while he looks for a different job. Burnout has lessened his patience and he is now short-tempered with his staff and congregants. He has also missed multiple days of work, even after using all of his paid time off (PTO). His staff and congregants do not understand the change in his behavior and begin to complain to one another as well as to board members. In this simple example, we see decreased congregant satisfaction, inappropriate behavior, absenteeism, and increased complaints.

Burnout negatively affects an entire organization or church. How does burnout affect the individual? Why did Pastor Tim do those things stated in the previous paragraph? Burnout affects the individual in two broad senses: (1) physical and (2) psychological/mental. From a physical standpoint, individuals living with burnout can experience cardiovascular disease, musculoskeletal disorders, psychological disorders, workplace injury, suicide, cancer, ulcers, and impaired immune function (Sauter et al., 1999). Individuals living with burnout may also experience sleep disturbances, headaches, gastrointestinal upset, and raised blood pressure/cardiovascular disease. In conjunction with these physical effects, burnout perpetuates psychological/mental consequences. A study conducted by the University of Cambridge (2011) revealed such consequences as anxiety, irritability, depression, and labile emotions; intellectual issues including loss of concentration, lack of motivation, difficulty with thought processes, loss of memory, and poor decision-making; and behavioral concerns such as isolation and unpunctuality.

We now understand that the pastor is affected from both a physical standpoint and a psychological/mental standpoint. We have also seen how a church, both employees and congregants, are affected by pastoral burnout. As such, it is important to note that burnout is not just an individual/pastor problem. Yes, the pastor experiencing burnout takes the brunt of negative consequences; however, these consequences of burnout often play out in the work environment, with congregants, and in the pastor's home life.

3

Emotional Labor and Burnout

Introduction

As MEMBERS OF THE helping profession (those who work with a person's physical, psychological, intellectual, emotional, or spiritual well-being) in the service industry, pastors find themselves in a unique role. This position requires that pastors wear many hats in order to successfully navigate their various duties. Pastors may have what seems like endless responsibilities on their plate including administrative, discipleship, and spiritual care. In any given week, pastors may preach and conduct worship services, supervise ministry teams, develop new programs, visit congregants in the hospital, lead Bible study, act as counsel to members of the church who are in crisis, and of course care for the spiritual health of their congregants. Their hours are not limited to the traditional eight to five, but rather it can feel as though they are on call all day, every day.

By profession and conviction, pastors must lead their flocks, but also simultaneously be part of the flock. In order to care for members of their church, pastors must establish relationships with those whom they shepherd. Doing so is crucial for the development of mutual trust and a level of intimacy that is necessary for the work being done. However, pastors may find that the nature of these relationships are a double-edged sword. When pastors care for and invest in relationships with a congregant, it allows them to walk next to that person. This intimacy enriches the experience, which helps to bear fruit, but an unintended consequence may be that pastors also end up taking their work home with them. Relationships after all are not just a file or document that can be saved and stored for a later time. Rather, congregants become people pastors love and care about and as such are difficult to leave "at work" when the day ends. As such, there could be spillover effects when pastors continue to think about the spiritual care of their congregants after "work hours."

As pastoring is an emotionally intensive profession, pastors must engage in a concept known as *emotional labor*, an unspoken workplace demand that has been the forefront of social psychological research for over fifty years. In this chapter, we will describe the concept of emotional labor, discuss emotional labor strategies used while on the job, and begin to examine the connection between emotional labor and the experience of pastoral burnout.

Emotional Labor and the Service Professions

When the American economy shifted from the production of goods to the delivery of services, sociologist Arlie Hochschild sought to make sense of the nature and consequences of service work (Wharton, 2009). By studying flight attendants in the 1970s, Hochschild developed the idea of "emotion work" to refer to the way people actively shape and direct their feelings based on what is expected of them in the situation. She argued that there are "feeling rules" or societal norms about the appropriate type and amount of feeling that should be experienced and expressed in a particular situation (Wharton, 2009). Hochschild noted that service work was unique in that employees are required to exert a certain level of emotional competence while on the job. "The emotion with which service is delivered is a major contributor to service quality"

(Huppertz et al., 2020, p. 214). In order to deliver services with the appropriate emotion, employees engage in *emotional labor*, which can be understood as the modification of emotional expression as part of the work role. For example, in customer service, salespeople are expected to smile and behave politely, even when a customer is being difficult. Emotional labor, then, is the act of expressing socially desired emotions during service transactions, despite the pleasantness or disagreeableness of the customer. Specifically, it is the management of feelings to create a publicly observable facial and bodily display which are often called nonverbal aspects of communication, which is then tacitly or implicitly provided as part of the wage and therefore has exchange value (Hochschild, 1983). This definition characterizes service providers as being required to manage their emotions and display those emotions for commercial purposes. In other words, service workers' feelings (at least while they are on the job) are commodified to align with the expectations of the organization for which they work.[1]

The concept of emotional labor is particularly relevant for employees in the service sector because they must manage their feelings and display those emotions as part of their job requirement (Shankar & Kumar, 2014). Emotions that are displayed while on the job then have economic value, which is then translated into salaries, wages, customer satisfaction surveys, and/or tips (Choi & Kim, 2015). According to Hochschild (1983, 2012) jobs involving emotional labor have three criteria: (1) they require face-to-face or voice-to-voice contact with the public; (2) they must have some organizational or professional display rules; and (3) they must induce a favorable emotional state. These attempts to change the intensity or quality of feelings to bring them into line with the requirements of the occasion are forms of emotion management and are seen as an integral aspect of the employee's job performance. However, what happens when workers are simply not feeling the socially desired emotions? For example, imagine that a pastor is

---

1. There is a psychological literature that distinguishes between feelings and emotions. For our purposes, we are following a more popular approach in making feelings and emotions synonyms.

meeting with a congregant who has just shared that he or she is engaging in sinful behavior. The pastor is shocked, perhaps even angered by the revelation, but he has to work to hide his initial reaction to the news.

Service workers who do not feel the required emotions may need to engage in one of the two emotional labor strategies: *surface acting* or *deep acting*. In some situations, it is considered advantageous to evoke an emotion that is currently absent or beyond what one is authentically feeling. At other times, emotion work or emotion management involves suppressing an emotion that is deemed inappropriate to the situation. Whereas surface acting only changes the expression of emotion, deep acting transforms our emotional state (Larson & Yao, 2005). To better understand the distinction between surface acting and deep acting, we can use the metaphor of an actor preparing for and performing in a show.

Emotional Labor Strategies

The first strategy used to regulate emotions while on the job is coined as *surface acting*. Surface acting involves simulating emotions that are not actually felt, by changing outward appearances (i.e., facial expression, gestures, or voice tone) when exhibiting the required emotions. In other words, the non-verbal aspects of communicating emotion do not reflect one's inner experience in the moment. Instead, surface acting means that the actor in the situation displays the correct emotion based on the social context despite not feeling that emotion. In this way, the actual or authentic feelings are not adjusted to match the inner experience, but instead emotions are feigned to align with the requirements of the job or the expectations of the situation. Surface acting can best be understood as a performance for the benefit of the audience. Using this technique, the worker or employee uses the setting, appearance, and manner to his advantage to put on a convincing show. One method used to evoke favorable emotions and suppress unfavorable ones is to adopt an appropriate physical posture (DeLamater et al., 2014). Surface acting is essentially displaying emotions that are not actually being felt in that moment.

Consider the following situation: A congregant named Sally has approached her pastor citing marital issues for which she is in counseling. In her meeting with her pastor, Sally brings forth concerns about her husband. While listening to Sally, her pastor begins to feel that Sally may be the one contributing to the marital discord, rather than her husband. However, her pastor is careful to control his facial expressions, gestures, and voice tone to ensure Sally feels as though he is listening to her and empathizing with the concerns she has brought forth. In short, her pastor is not displaying his true feelings toward Sally, but rather he is displaying the feelings considered appropriate for the situation. Subsequently, Sally leaves the meeting feeling heard and understood, with a plan of action for working on her marriage.

Another illustration of surface acting can be seen in a recent conversation with a pastor of a mid-sized church. He spoke of the challenges the church faced during the height of the global pandemic. While recounting the events, he shared that a congregant was upset that the church was following state guidelines for in-person services. He recalled that the congregant came to his home unannounced and began yelling at him through his door while his wife and children were present. Of the event he said, "I felt as though I were being clipped. I couldn't respond the way I wanted to. I couldn't give him a piece of my mind. I had a duty to be an image bearer. I had to have a sense of grace." In this situation, the pastor had to put a great deal of effort into forcing a calm demeanor despite the frustration he was feeling internally.

A second strategy used to regulate emotions while on the job is known as *deep acting*. Deep acting, on the other hand, is when a worker or employee attempts to actually experience or feel the emotions that they wish to display. In deep acting, a feeling or emotional response is self-induced, and the feeling provides the basis of acting. Here a service worker psychs him/herself into experiencing the desired emotions (Ashforth & Humphrey, 1993). In other words, the feelings are actively adjusted so that the underlying emotions that are felt and displayed are aligned with the required or expected emotions of the situation (Grandey, 2000). In other words, deep acting reflects the emotional effort to cultivate the desired feeling and authentically express it. Deep acting can be achieved through a couple ways; "one is by directly exhorting a feeling, the other by making indirect use of a trained imagination" (Hochschild, 2012, p. 38). Specifically, workers either try to stir up feelings they wish they had or, alternatively, they try to block or weaken a feeling they wish they did not have. In deep acting, workers also set a personal stage with props, not for the benefit of the audience, but to help them to believe in what it is they are experiencing. This can include friends, coworkers, or acquaintances who influence their feelings in a desired direction. Unlike surface acting, deep acting involves changing one's inner feelings by altering more than the outward appearance. In surface acting, feelings are changed from the "outside in," whereas in deep acting, feelings are changed from the "inside out" (Hochschild, 1983).

Consider the following scenario: Michael meets with his pastor to share that his father just passed away and he is having trouble coping with the loss. He has spiraled into a deep depression and cannot muster the energy to care for his young daughter. His pastor was surprised that Michael's father had passed but didn't think his emotions accurately reflected the bad news. Michael was understandably upset, so the pastor tried to really focus on his emotional state and began to picture images of losing his own father. In that moment he empathized with Michael and developed an authentic feeling of grief and in doing so was able to shore up the correct intensity of sadness for the sake of better relating to helping Michael process his loss during his time of need.

In another scenario, a pastor is meeting with the church elders. The church elders are expressing concern over congregants leaving the church. The pastor, who has observed this week after week, understands the concerns of those that are leaving, but is himself feeling too weary to initiate action. In order to muster the proper sense of urgency to match the church elders, the pastor listens raptly and begins to internalize these concerns as being both important and valid. By the end of the meeting, the pastor feels a renewed sense of purpose to help with recruiting and retainment efforts.

Emotional Labor and Burnout

We have established that emotional labor is a necessary component of service work and even more foundational for helping professions (e.g., doctors, nurses, teachers, pastors, etc.). What happens when service workers engage in emotional labor day in and day out? Researchers have found that there are harmful effects of both surface acting and deep acting on the service worker (Hochschild, 1983; Grandey, 2000). The relationship between surface acting and negative outcomes is consistent and clear. Namely, surface acting has been found to be strongly and positively related to work strain and emotional exhaustion (Huppertz et al., 2020). Specifically, it has been found that portraying emotions that are not felt (as in the case of surface acting) creates a sense of tension that is termed emotive dissonance (Hochschild, 1983). This concept refers to the conflict between experienced emotions and emotions expressed to conform to display rules. According to Wharton (2009), numerous studies show that workers who report having to display emotions that conflict with their own feelings on a regular basis are more likely than others to experience emotional exhaustion, which is related to burnout. For example, imagine that a pastor has had a particularly late night visiting with a congregant who has fallen ill. He wakes up Sunday morning exhausted, but he is responsible for giving the sermon. As he is giving the sermon, he acts lively and energetic, despite feeling spent. He is engaging in surface acting and over time this emotive dissonance he experiences could lead to personal and work-related maladjustment such as poor self-esteem, depression, and cynicism.

While the connection between surface acting and exhaustion is quite clear and consistent, the relationship between deep acting and negative outcomes has been mixed. On the one hand, in typical service jobs, deep acting requires changing one's underlying emotions into a more positive one so that the display requirements are met. Under conditions where the situation calls for positive display rules, workers can actually experience more positive emotions when using deep acting. Therefore, the effort workers place into actually creating these feelings within themselves is compensated in some way, perhaps by positive interactions (Huppertz et al., 2020). In these situations, research has found that deep acting can actually lead to positive feelings and a reduction of negative feelings (Lennard et al., 2019; Scott & Barnes, 2011). On the other hand, regularly engaging in deep acting may distort authentic emotional reactions and impair one's sense of authentic self, thereby impairing one's well-being. Deep acting, then, may also lead to self-alienation as one loses touch with their authentic self, which could impair one's ability to recognize or experience real emotions over time (Ashforth, 1989).

While there are many consequences for engaging in emotional labor, one that we focus on throughout this book is burnout, and, specifically, pastoral burnout. One of the causes of burnout occurs when workers are unable to maintain sufficient psychological distance between the emotional requirements of their job and their sense of self (Shankar & Kumar, 2014). It is a result of the stress experienced by the individuals, and anything causing stress and tension is thought to have an effect upon burnout. Burnout research implies that burnout is not an individual stress response, but rather is related to an individual's relational transactions in the workplace. With respect to emotional labor, surface acting was found to be related to such stress outcomes (Brotheridge & Lee, 1998; Brotheridge, 1999; Erickson & Wharton, 1997; Pugliesi & Shook, 1997), whereas deep acting, was found to be related to a greater sense of personal efficacy of work (Brotheridge & Lee, 1998). Interaction with people, besides leading to fatigue, requires the regulation of emotions and is thought to trigger burnout (Rafaeli & Sutton, 1989). In a study conducted by Zapf (2002), it was reported that there is a positive correlation between emotional labor and burnout. Translated in lay terms, this means that studies show greater engagement in emotional labor increases the experience of burnout. As another example, Brotheridge and Grandey (2002) discovered a correlation between emotional exhaustion and the need to prevent negative feelings. As such, workers employed in the categories of "high emotional labor" jobs (Hochschild, 1983) and "high burnout jobs" (Cordes & Dougherty, 1993) report significantly higher levels of stress than do other workers. Specifically, occupants of health care, social service, teaching, and other "caring" professions are more likely to experience burnout (Cherniss, 1993; Jackson et al., 1986; Leiter & Maslach, 1988; Schaufeli et al., 1993).

The consequences of burnout are far reaching. Maslach and Leiter (1997) found that burnout can cause depleted energy and emotional exhaustion, lowered resistance to illness, increased depersonalization in interpersonal relationships, increased dissatisfaction and pessimism, and increased absenteeism and reduced work efficiency. Burnout among the pastorate has become increasingly prevalent over the years, but few are acknowledging the severity of the problem. In speaking with a director of a national ministry which seeks to serve struggling pastors, he admitted: "The problem (of burnout) is getting worse. It's to the point where pastors come to us and say, the only way I can get out of this is if I'm dead." One pastor of a large church confessed, "I was having so many conversations with people in my ministry who needed me. I recall one week during the pandemic, I had over one hundred conversations! I realized I was burned out when I lost energy to play with my kids. I didn't even want to have conversations with my wife anymore." When asked what resources were available to him, he said: "There's a lot of unawareness in the church about what to do or how to do it. Counseling is available for others, but it's not for me. There's a stigma. It's not seen as a problem until the whole house is on fire." In addressing the experiences of burnout that stemmed from political and social tensions in his church, another pastor recounted, "People who I walked with were leaving the church. It was really hard for me. Emotionally, I was a wreck. I wasn't sleeping. I have an auto-immune disorder and it was getting worse, barely manageable at that point. It was hard to let go of some of the bitterness I had towards some people and fight against that. Under the suggestion of the church elders, I took a sabbatical, which was good for me, but we also lost a lot of people during that time, which was painful due to our size. When I came back, however, the old feelings just resurfaced. Lately, I have been questioning if I'm called to pastor anymore. I'm no longer sure it's doable."

Understanding the concept of emotional labor, emotional labor regulation strategies, and the relationship between emotional labor and burnout are key as it demonstrates that burnout is not caused by individual deficiencies, failings, or flaws. Burnout, as we have come to understand it, is a very real consequence of engaging in emotional labor, which happens to be a critical requirement of the pastoral profession.

4

Work and Family Balance

Introduction

PASTORS OFTEN FACE EXTREMELY difficult decisions as they minister in their churches along with living in their communities with their families. Living and working in the same community alongside one's family often places ministers in socially complicated relationships with both. What happens when the phone rings during family dinner time? Is the call an emergency? Is it from the congregant that is facing an extreme personal crisis like the impending death of a family member? Or is this another call to complain about the sermon from Sunday? What happens when these calls and other interruptions occur during important family events? Does the minister leave his or her child's graduation to be with a congregant in need? Does the minister miss senior night for his or her child's high school sport?

Lest we villainize the local church, sometimes these tensions derive from the family side. Perhaps the pastor's children frequently get in trouble at church or cause mischief during Sunday school. What happens when the pastor's spouse engages in conflict with other families in the congregation? What happens when the minster's family complains that the minister spends more time with the church than with them? All these time, support, and behavior demands increase the stress on ministers and their families.

Often the usual interpersonal boundaries that non-minister families take for granted are violated or transgressed (see Cameron Lee and colleagues' work on this: Lee, 1995, 1999; Lee & Iverson-Gilbert, 2003). In other words, most service providers have at least some separations between their work and family life. Social workers, marriage and family therapists, and counselors can separate their family lives from their work lives. These service providers can leave work at the office and unplug from stressful work environments. Minsters do not usually have that luxury. The minister and family live and worship in the community alongside the congregation. Cameron Lee and Jack Balswick (2006) describe this as living in a glass house. The glass house metaphor describes how the congregation is privy to the inner workings of the minister's family. Consequently, this increases the stress on the minister and family as they live out their calling. Further, the accessibility of living in the community facilitates intrusions, Lee calls these ministry demands, between work and family life.

The minister's family is in a unique social context due to the embedded and embodied nature of congregational ministry. The minister's family finds itself living in the primary vocational context of the pastor, and this sometimes results in significant conflict and stress. When there is an issue within the family, say, between the minister and his spouse, the congregation, or at least parts of the congregation, are aware of it. The same goes for any parenting issues. The congregation has a special vantage point to observe and to some extent live alongside the minister that other careers and vocations do not afford. The result is often increased stress on the part of the minister and the family. Sometimes this heightened sense of access results in hiding one's problems from others and not seeking help.

Burnout and Work and Family Domains

As we have learned more about the experiences and causes of burnout, the focus has turned to the interface between work and family life. Burnout is not only an individual's experience due to work related strain and stress, but is also based on the interaction of many important life contexts. In other words, work and family life have a complex relationship—sometimes these spheres of life are in conflict, sometimes they are supportive. Conflict and burnout result from the mismatch between an individual's roles in the separate spheres of work and family. Often these conflictual relationships focus on time, strain, and behavior (Greenhaus & Beutell, 1985).

Role conflict may be thought of as occurring because *time demands* are made in the separate spheres of work and family. That is, both the family and work spheres make demands on the time, energy, resources, and skills of the individual. For pastors, these demands may occur at any time and for any reason. These time demands usually occur as one parent/spouse is at work and away from the family. Work most obviously demands a physical presence away from home, while the family's demands often occur as intrusions for work—a child's doctor's appointment, a parent-teacher conference during the daytime, a call from the spouse that the refrigerator is leaking. Ministry demands are intrusive on a pastor's family unlike other careers or vocations (Lee, 1999). As a pastor and family living in the church community, there is a blurring of any distinction between these life contexts. Time demands work differently in the pastor's life. The pastor's time at work as a minister is embedded in the family's life in the church community. There is little separation between work and family time for the pastor. The congregation may make time demands of the pastor during times that are usually considered family time in other vocations. On top of this, the family may have difficulty in maintaining unique time for one another as a result of living in the church community.

Psychological strain may occur as a result of the conflict between work and family life. This is essentially the focus of the way researchers understand burnout. Emotional exhaustion, an aspect of psychological strain, is usually the main component used to explain this experience (see Maslach et al., 2001; Frederick et al., 2018). The focus of emotional exhaustion is the emptiness, lethargy, lack of care, and spiritual dryness associated with the depletion of psychological resources. This experience has been described as the emptiness of *acedia* (Frederick et al., 2018). Acedia describes the experience of both *apathy*—a loss of care for others—as well as being *indifferent* to the needs of others. Pastors experiencing burnout often experience apathy and indifference for congregants and their own families as a result of the strain of inter-role conflict.

Behavior focuses on the separate actions needed at work and home. Often adults act differently whether they are working or at home. Conflicts may arise when home behavior is done at work or vice versa. For pastors, home life is lived in the work context. The ambiguity associated with living out one's family life in the context of the congregation increases conflict due to the behaving as if at work or home depending on who is around. The pastor is constantly faced with questions—How do I discipline my children? Will I be viewed as too lenient or too harsh? What happens if I get into an argument with my spouse? What happens if a congregant argues with me as the pastor? How do I respond? What will my spouse and children think about a church member being angry with me?

Types of Relationships between Work and Family Life

Researchers have described several types of relationships to help understand the complicated ways in which work and family life interface. The first view on the relationship between work and family is one of *conflict* (Allen & Martin, 2017; Greenhaus & Beutell, 1985). Work and family conflict (WFC) is conceptualized as conflict between incompatible demands regarding role pressure and expectations in work and family domains. That is, WFC is caused when pressure in one domain, say the family, interferes with or puts demands on workplace obligations. As an example, a pastor may face significant stress when he realizes that the small group leader meeting has been scheduled on the same night as his only daughter's piano recital. How is this time demand conflict resolved? Does the pastor skip the meeting for the recital? Does the recital get skipped? What is the emotional cost for the family for missing the recital? What about the church's expectations regarding the need for the pastor to attend these types of events? Psychological strain due to work and family conflict may have significant negative consequences. Prolonged levels of work to family conflict may even lead to family dissolution and impact childbearing and childrearing (Burch, 2020). WFC focuses on the negative aspects of the relationship between work and family domains.

Work and family spheres may provide more positive or mutually enhancing or *enriching* resources for individuals (Allen & Martin, 2017). That is, individuals may develop important skills, experiences, and resources in one domain, say family life, that are transferable to the other domain, say work. These enriching resources are usually grouped into five general types (Greenhaus and Powell, 2006): skills and perspectives, psychological and physical resources, social-capital resources, flexibility, and material resources. These resources provide both instrumental (skills and abilities that are directly transferable across domains) as well as emotional resources. For example, workers that experience support from their families, i.e., someone in the family tries to understand when he or she is having difficulty at work, is related to increased job satisfaction (which is called a spillover effect), and work-related support for one's family is also associated with job satisfaction (a direct effect) (Zhang et al., 2018).

People tend to emphasize the need for *balance* between work and family (Allen & Martin, 2017; Grzywacz & Carlson, 2007). At its most general level, work-family balance has been defined as: "accomplishment of role-related expectations that are negotiated and shared between an individual and his or her role-related partners in the work and family domains" (Grzywacz & Carlson, 2007, p. 458). Individuals feel work and family life are balanced when there is a level of negotiation regarding how and when tasks are accomplished. The emphasis on accomplishment of expectations emphasizes the social embeddedness of work and family (and potential conflict) and the resolution of that conflict or achievement of personal goals. One of the benefits of this definition is the focus on expectations. That is, this definition moves beyond one's subjective appraisal—feelings of satisfaction—regarding achieving a balance in work and family domains. Balance is not about how the individual feels about the relationship between work and family life. Instead, the individual must also consider how well he or she is performing in each domain in meeting expectations and accomplishing tasks. In other words, balance is based on social context and meeting one's expectations of work and family life.

Kalliath and Brough (2008) describe six other definitions of work-family balance (WFB). These six definitions are: (1) work-family balance as focused on multiple roles, (2) equality across multiple roles, (3) satisfaction between multiple roles, (4) salience of fulfillment of multiple roles, (5) balance as the relationship between conflict and facilitation or enrichment across multiple roles, and (6) perceived control between multiple roles. Definition one emphasizes that individuals have multiple roles to fulfill in various life domains like work and the family. The multiple role emphasis focuses on how both domains, work and family, are mutually influencing one another which may facilitate or enhance growth in either or both domains. Unfortunately, this influence may also produce conflict. Defining WFB as equality emphasizes the need for sharing of time and behavior demands across the domains of work and family. The third definition of WFB emphasizes the perceptions of satisfaction in these domains. That is, the individual is satisfied with each role thus minimizing inter-role conflict. Salience of roles emphasizes the relative impact of role demands and how these change throughout an individual's life. WFB has also been defined as low levels of conflict and high levels of enrichment between work and family. The final definition of WFB focuses on

Work and Family Balance

the role autonomy or personal choice over time, strain, and behavior demands across work and family domains.

Table 1. Work and Family Balance Domains.

Type of Balance	Experience in multiple roles	Equality in roles	Satisfaction in roles	Salience in roles	Ratio of conflict and enrichment	Perceived control
Subjective	Acknowledgment that individual occupies many roles.	Individual determines how equal domains are. Not based on time committed in either domain.	An individual feels satisfied in either or both domains.	Individual decides which domain is most important.	No.	An individual feels that he or she exercises some control over demands from work and family.
Objective	No.				The amount of strain due to time, resources, and behavior is measured against enrichment.	
Negotiated	No.	Yes.	No.	No.	Yes	No.

Table 1 describes WFB relationships. The benefit of focusing on more objective approaches is that there is a basis for evaluating the conflict between work and family life. Relying on personal satisfaction and personal salience (and perceived control) means that WFB may change dramatically from moment to moment making any enrichment unlikely. That is, if one's view of WFB is based on an emotional evaluation of that relationship, due to the ebbs and flows of life at work and home, no consistent enrichment may occur. In fact, WFB can be experienced as joy in the morning and the depths of despair by evening! However, individuals need to have some control over (1) how demands are addressed in the two spheres of work and family life (actual control based in evaluating the salience of the demands) (2) that are negotiated between the spheres, (3) entail the accomplishing of tasks from each domain, and (4) result in satisfaction in each domain.

In combining all these different definitions and emphases of WFB, it can be thought of as *salience and satisfaction* based in the domains of work and family life. Frederick and Dunbar define it this way: "WFB *[is] one's perception of the compatibility and enhancing nature of both work and non-work activities in accordance with one's values and preferences*" (2019, p. 23). This definition combines the focus on the social context or embeddedness of WFB (Grzywacz & Carlson, 2007) while maintaining the need for evaluating the accomplishment of tasks for WFB, i.e., satisfaction. Further, WFB is often based on the level of control or perceived control in managing expectations and demands from each domain which is included in the processes for discerning salience.

Salience and satisfaction summarize this definition of WFB. Salience refers to the importance of one domain compared to the other, while satisfaction refers to one's evaluation of well-being in either domain. Individuals need the ability to discern which domain is more important at any given time. Satisfaction in either domain spills over into the other domain when there are pressures and tension. For example, Pastor Tim is new to his congregation as he has only been there three months. While acclimating to his new community, Pastor Tim and his wife decide to enroll their ten-year-old into soccer. Pastor Tim experiences role conflict as he tries to achieve balance between the congregation's demands and his family's demands. Pastor Tim receives a call that a member needs him while on the way to his daughter's first soccer match of the season. How does Pastor Tim manage these demands? How does he determine which domain, work or family, is most salient at that moment? How successful or satisfied is Pastor Tim as a pastor and father at that moment?

Family Systems and WFB

One of the most robust resources provided by one's family of origin (FOO) for managing burnout is Differentiation of Self (DoS). In other words, DoS is a significant family resource for the workplace. It contributes to how pastors may discern the salience of congregational and familial demands while experiencing satisfaction in one domain despite conflict from the other. DoS may be conceptualized along two dimensions (Frederick & Dunbar, 2019). First, DoS has an intrapersonal dimension. Intrapersonal DoS describes one's ability to acknowledge and purposefully respond in a values-based manner to one's inner experience. This means that individuals with high levels of DoS are able to identify inner experiences, sometimes that arise as responses to stressful relationships and social contexts, and respond to those experiences in a values-based or identity-informed manner. That is, intrapersonal DoS is a level of emotional maturity that fosters responding in appropriate and value-driven ways to one's experiences. This is an emotional regulation function.

The interpersonal dimension of DoS focuses on the ability to maintain relationships with others while maintaining one's values-based identity commitments. That is, interpersonal DoS describes the ability to remain connected with others while remaining authentic to one's identity, even in the face of extreme emotional pressure to maintain the relationship at the cost of identity. An example of this based on Pastor Tim's experience at his daughter's first soccer game described above focuses on how Pastor Tim could minimize or ignore the emotional tension of having to either ignore the church *or* his daughter to maintain his identity as either a pastor *or* a father. Interpersonal DoS would describe Pastor Tim's ability to remain both a pastor and a father in his relationships with the congregation and his daughter despite the emotional pressure to choose either one or the other identity and relationship.

DoS is the psychological resource, derived and developed in one's FOO, that facilitates salience and satisfaction. As demonstrated in figure 2, DoS provides the concrete skills to manage the emotional strain derived from work and family due to its emotion regulation function. That is, intrapersonal DoS enables the individual to withstand and process intense demands from both work and family domains without losing one's sense of identity and belonging. As part of this process, one is able to separate one's identity from one's work and family roles. This skill is crucial for coping with pastoral burnout. Role differentiation allows pastors to distinguish their personal identity from that of being a pastor, allowing them to experience satisfaction in other dimensions of identity.

Interpersonal DoS provides the resources to maintain relationships with family and work despite the emotional stressors coming from each domain. As discernment allows one to more objectively evaluate the relative importance of demands coming from a specific domain, relationships with each domain are maintained even when deciding that a specific demand is not as crucial or pressing at a specific time.

Figure 2. Differentiation and WFB.

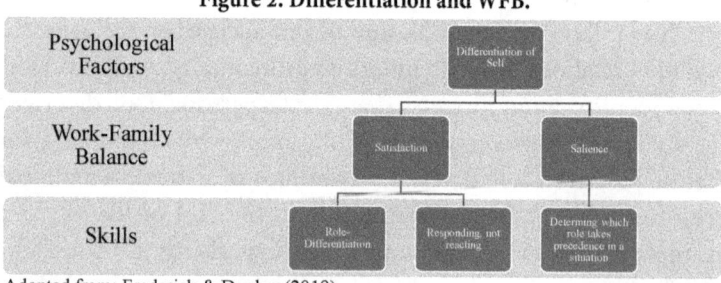

Adopted from: Frederick & Dunbar (2019).

In returning to Pastor Tim's situation, he is able to discern the relative demands of being present for his daughter's first soccer match of the year and the congregant's needs. As part of this discernment, Pastor Tim should determine the level of need from both his daughter and the congregant. Does the congregant need the pastor for spiritual support in a serious emergency, or is the congregant wanting the pastor to decide which automobile color to choose? For the daughter, how important is her dad's presence at the soccer game to her? DoS fosters Pastor Tim's ability to manage the stressors associated with the congregant and daughter while maintaining connection to both. Additionally, DoS allows Pastor Tim to discern the salience of both spheres' demands and respond accordingly.

Chapter 4 described the interpersonal nature of burnout and how burnout is often due to conflict between family and work roles. However, conflict is not the only type of relationship between work as described by WFB. We can think of how work and family domains could be mutually enriching, especially using the concept of differentiation of self. Differentiation allows individuals to determine the salience (or importance) of demands from work and family domains as well as experiencing satisfaction (or feelings of well-being) in each.

5

Pastoral Burnout

Introduction

CHAPTER 5 WILL DESCRIBE Cameron Lee's research (Lee & Balswick, 2006) on ministry demands and boundary violations (*Life in a Glass House* metaphor) and their contribution to work and family balance with the pastorate. Lee describes the pastor's family as being in a unique social context, which may contribute greatly to burnout due to work and family conflict. Pastoral burnout will also be described using Francis's (Francis et al., 2017; Francis et al., 2019; Francis et al., 2011) definition of pastoral burnout. One of Francis's main contributions focuses on understanding how pastors tend to report high levels of burnout yet remain in ministry. Finally, chapter 5 will present our DifC model for coping with burnout as a pastor.

Life in a Glass House

The vocation of ministry provides one of the most unique social contexts for any career as the pastor's family can live close in proximity to where the pastor works as well as spend much of their time in the church. That is, the usual boundary between work and family does not exist for the pastor and family. The pastor, the pastor's family, and the congregation all do life together. This social location regarding the career of pastors presents a challenge when thinking about pastoral burnout. With the pastor's family and the congregation living together, the overlapping and ambiguous nature of their relationship presents opportunities for pastors to experience increased stress from both the family and congregation. This stress comes from experiencing demands for time, energy, and resources from the congregation and family.

Cameron Lee (1995; Lee & Balswick, 1989) describes the social boundary between the pastor and family as being ambiguous. Most career paths see a distinct separation between the worker and his or her family. The social boundaries between the pastor's family and the congregation are fluid as there is more overlap in terms of time, availability, and membership. The pastor and the family live amid the congregation. This means the pastor lives in a glass house along with the family. There are often unspoken expectations regarding how the pastor raises his or her family. Further, there are expectations on participation in the life of the congregation other church members don't have. The expectations are experienced as demands. The pastor's family experiences demand from the congregation. Sometimes these demands are for participation in specific ministries. Sometimes these demands are behavioral expectations. This means the pastor and family experience increased stress due to living with the congregation.

The pastor's membership in their own family is also ambiguous. This means the family knows that the pastor is physically present, but they have a difficult time counting on his availability to perform spousal and parenting duties. The family experiences stress when a parent or spouse dies, and their membership is removed from the family. This stress causes the family to readjust to the absence of the member. In the pastor's situation, he is still alive and part of the family. However, given the demands of the congregation, the pastor may forego important obligations to the family. When the congregation makes a demand, many times the pastor interrupts family time in order to minister to the flock. We describe some of these demands in the example below.

Francis and the Study of Pastoral Burnout

Understanding the nature of burnout is crucial to how we develop strategies to cope with it. There has been an increasing concern that the main ways we study burnout do not adequately reflect the experience of pastors (Frederick et al., 2023). The main concerns with current research are (1) the focus on exhaustion as being the main experience of burnout, and (2) the persistence of pastors in high stress ministry despite experiencing high levels of emotional exhaustion.

The main way burnout is assessed is using the Maslach Burnout Inventory, called the MBI (Maslach et al., 1996). The MBI consists of three subscales measuring exhaustion, depersonalization, and professional efficacy. These have been described in some detail in chapter 2. We want to emphasize here that emotional exhaustion has been identified as the main component of burnout. Exhaustion has been incorporated into most of the other tools used to research burnout. Tools like the Francis Burnout Inventory (Francis et al., 2017) and the Copenhagen Burnout Inventory (Kristensen et al., 2005) all use exhaustion or emotional exhaustion to describe the personal experience of it. Frederick (et al., 2023) continues: "Common among all such instruments are questions designed to measure exhaustion. Words such as fatigue, worn-out, energy, tired, weary, and drained are found on the aforementioned burnout measurement instruments" (p. 123).

This leads us to the second concern: Why do pastors persist in ministries when experiencing high levels of exhaustion or burnout? Francis (Francis et al., 2017; Francis et al., 2019; Francis et al., 2011) describes how pastoral burnout should consider the emotional toll of ministry while considering the meaningfulness of ministry. His approach to understanding pastoral burnout views burnout as a ratio between the emotional exhaustion or tool of ministry compared to the meaningfulness of ministry. This notion captures the idea that pastoral ministry is stressful and emotionally draining yet pastors experience a level of meaningfulness that provides support for remaining in stressful occupations. Pastors may persist in highly stressful ministries because these ministries are meaningful. The sense of importance provides pastors with resources needed to cope with exhaustion in ministry.

Francis's research is supported by our research on pastors. We will discuss our approach using Differentiation in Christ (DifC) below. However, Francis's focus on meaningfulness in ministry identifies a core component of pastoral work—the purpose of it. Pastors are called into ministry, and this call transforms the nature and meaning of ministry. Given the call of God into ministry, there is in inherent meaningfulness of the work. God is the source and purpose of pastoring, and this purpose should inform how pastors live out their calling. Pastoring reflects both the reason of the ministry as well as the purpose—shepherding the flock. That is, God creates the ground for pastoring. God is also the purpose. Pastoring is pointing others to become more like God in Christ. The pastor is called to be the shepherd and point his flock to the Good Shepherd (Rinne, 2014).

Pastors are able to cope with the exhaustion of being with and for the congregation because the work is meaningful. The focus in Francis's work is the personal meaningfulness of work. The pastor derives a personal sense that ministry is important, purposeful, and satisfying. In our view, meaningfulness is more than a personal identification with, or experience of, satisfaction with ministry. Francis asks pastors about their perceptions of the meaningfulness of work. One of the items on Francis's Satisfaction in Ministry Scale reads, "I have accomplished many worthwhile things in my current ministry" (Village et al., 2018, p. 97).This item demonstrates the personal, subjective notion of attributing meaningfulness and satisfaction with ministry as opposed to the sense of calling imbibing ministry with purpose. In other words, we would highlight the calling components of the pastorate while Francis speaks of the personal meaningfulness of ministry.

Differentiation in Christ and Pastoral Burnout

DifC—Differentiation in Christ—provides the psychological and spiritual resources needed to prevent and cope with pastoral burnout. As pastoral burnout is a spiritual depletion of resources regarding the experience of God's calling on our lives as both his children and as his ministers vocationally, DifC fosters invigorating our *identities* in terms of calling using spiritual disciplines. DifC as an identity is based primarily on God's effectual call on our lives (Frederick & Dunbar, 2022). That is, we are called and received as adopted members into Christ's family. We become Christians based on Christ's saving work on the cross. This is the primary call on our lives and identities.

The primary calling on our lives is expressed via our secondary sets of callings. That is, we live out our identities as Christ's brothers and sisters vocationally. We are called to work. We are called to be married and parents. We are called to serve in various ways in our lives. All these secondary calls are opportunities to express our primary identities—as children of God in Christ.

DifC enables us to live our primary call or identity with the social and vocational worlds in which we live. DifC is the values-based, Christian view, that who we are is meditated in Christ's work on the cross. Further, DifC provides the values- or identity-based resources to authentically reflect our call as a Christian in our vocations. Our identity in Christ provides the core of who we are, and this core is expressed authentically as we live to glorify God in our vocations.

The two main tools DifC provides are satisfaction and salience (Frederick & Dunbar, 2019, 2022). Satisfaction refers to the esteem we receive as being children of God. We are reminded of Tim Keller's famous quote (Keller & Keller, 2016, p. 44): "The gospel is this: We are more sinful and flawed in ourselves than we ever dared believe, yet at the very same time we are more loved and accepted in Jesus Christ than we ever dared hope." The idea here is that our identities in Christ reflect both our need for forgiveness and the grace and forgiveness that Christ provides. In our primary call as Christians, we base our new identity as a beloved child of God. We have confidence in knowing our identity in Christ, and with this knowledge we can experience deep satisfaction, well-being, and acceptance. Our experience of satisfaction (what we could call our self-esteem) is based on the gospel call on our lives.

DifC and Satisfaction

We have confidence, safety, and an abiding security based in our calling as Christians. Our sense of self-esteem is enduring and accurate. That is, self-esteem based on behavior is often fleeting. As Jay Adams reminds us, self-esteem in secular view is often glorifying the self and its desires. "Plainly it is saying that self-esteem—a good self-image—is central to success in life, and, according to some, even in death" (Adams, 1986, p. 27). This focus is based on a high view of self, and it reflects how one's inner worth is based on achieving one's personal goals. Further, it is based on how others should reflect to the self its inherent goodness. That is, self-esteem is often based on how others praise us, not necessarily on our actual performance. For example, parents are encouraged to praise their children no matter what. Teachers praise all the efforts of their students. Pastors encourage the congregation, not admonish it.

Research suggests that individuals experience higher levels of self-esteem if they perceive themselves (1) as effectively engaging with their environments, (2) consistently acting in alignment with their values and identities, and (3) reflecting membership in specific social groups (Burke, 1991; Marcussen, 2006). You feel good about yourself when you are authentically living out your values, especially those that come from groups you identify with. The opposite is also true. You feel worse about yourself if you think that you are ineffective and are not living authentically to your values.

Christian self-esteem is based on our identity in Christ. Because Christ provides the foundation of our identity and membership in his eternal family, our identity is secure and safe. Further, this foundation is based on grace. We do not earn it. We cannot achieve it. It is Christ's love offering to us. As a response to Christ's graciousness, we do our best to live out this identity, and to the extent we accurately and authentically express this identity, consequently self-esteem increases. However, the basis of this self-esteem is founded on Christ. This foundation provides a reservoir of psychological resources crucial to supporting our continued expression of this identity in our secondary callings.

DifC is one way we describe this benefit. Our satisfaction with, our identity in, or our self-esteem embedded in our identity in Christ means that we have a solid sense of self from which we respond to others. When we experience challenges or threats to self-esteem based in our secondary calls, we do not need to be overwhelmed with negative experiences and self-appraisals. Instead, DifC provides psychological, identity-based resources to absorb or lessen the impact of those experiences. These processes will be described below in our example with Pastor Will and his family.

Professional literature identifies lowered self-efficacy and sense of purpose as components of the experience of burnout (Maslach & Leiter, 1997; Maslach et al., 2001). Francis and colleagues (Francis et al., 2017; Francis et al., 2019; Francis et al., 2011) developed this idea further by conceptualizing burnout for pastors along satisfaction with ministry lines. That is, professional efficacy takes on a specialized role in Francis's research. Pastors can withstand the emotional impact of depletion to the extent they view ministry as meaningful. Pastors who view their ministry as meaningful are able to endure increased experiences of emptiness, depletion, and emotional exhaustion due to ministry demands.

A significant source of pastoral burnout is due to the conflict experienced between the family and congregation (Lee, 1995, 2007; Lee & Balswick, 2006; Kim et al., 2016). When demands are made between these two secondary callings, pastors often experience a lowered view of personal effectiveness in these domains. That is, the pastor may begin to question his effectiveness as a pastor when receiving negative feedback from the congregation. This could be even worse if his family is also experiencing challenges.

When the pastor bases his identity on his role as either a pastor or father, this experience could deplete any sense of satisfaction. As a result, the pastor in this situation is especially vulnerable to pastoral burnout. However, a pastor with higher levels of DifC would have the psychological resources to absorb or manage the negativity coming from home or the congregation as his identity is in Christ. His satisfaction is founded on Christ's grace.

An Example

Pastor Will is in his third year of full-time ministry. This is his first pastoral ministry after graduating seminary, and he and his wife recently had their third child. The first two years of ministry were marked with some ministry successes where the congregation added twenty new members. It was also marked with some challenges as the congregation, under Pastor Will's leadership, implemented an elder/deacon model of church governance. In the process of this dual transition, bringing Pastor Will on and moving towards an elder-led model, the church split with one prominent family deciding to leave the congregation publicly and painfully.

Pastor Will came to the church three years ago confident in his call. He was experiencing a heightened sense of love of God as he completed seminary and received this first call. His family life was going well as he and his wife had welcomed two children during this time. He really felt like he was God's beloved. His self-esteem was high at this time.

As more and more conflict developed at the church, Pastor Will noticed that he was growing sadder and more lethargic. It was increasingly difficult for him to "feel" like God was close. Almost weekly, someone in the congregation would say or do something indicating they were critical of his ministry. The reservoir of self-esteem Pastor Will had from seminary was evaporating, and he did not know how to combat its depletion.

Pastor Will noticed an increasing distance in his marriage. His wife, Teresa, seemed to be more and more emotionally unavailable. They were arguing more than they ever had. Teresa began complaining that Will was never around; that every time someone in the church called, he would immediately go to them. Will was physically present for meals, but he was often silent and emotionally distant.

What we learned from talking with Pastor Will is that he was basing his self-esteem on his roles as a pastor and father/husband. When he was experiencing success in his roles, he would feel good about himself. When he was experiencing conflict, he would not feel so good about his identity as a pastor or father/husband. At the beginning of his ministry, he mainly experienced conflict with the congregation as they were trying to adjust to his leadership style and transition their church governance. It was during the second year of ministry when he began experiencing conflict with Teresa and his family. His satisfaction with his family and his roles in the family provided a self-esteem buffer to absorb some of the conflict from the congregation. When satisfaction in both roles is diminished, then his overall self-esteem, based on his roles, suffers. Consequently, he began experiencing burnout.

Pastor Will's experience of burnout reflected (1) a lowered sense of satisfaction in ministry as well as (2) increased emotional exhaustion. That is, the ministry became increasingly task oriented, and he was going through the motions in fulfilling his ministry obligations. He lost sight of the people he was ministering to, and they became tasks that he needed to complete. Further, he noticed that he was increasingly depleted. His spiritual life was dry and empty: he felt that God was distant and punishing. He felt he was unable to be there for his wife and family. He thought he was disappointing the congregation and that his ministry was pointless. He was losing his passion for life; he was losing his drive. Nothing meant anything to him anymore. He had no emotional space to be with his family nor his congregation. He viewed the people in his life as draining what precious emotional energy he had.

In situations like this, DifC may provide the necessary resources for Pastor Will to manage this conflict. Notice we said manage and not avoid. These types of conflicts are inevitable in the life of the pastor. DifC anchors Pastor Will's identity in who he is in Christ, and not in how he's acting like a Christian or fulfilling certain roles. DifC is based on the grace we receive as being called into God's family based on Jesus's saving work, not on anything we could do. In other words, DifC describes our immutable identity in Christ as the basis for anything we do on his behalf.

For Pastor Will, developing his identity based in DifC may provide him the resources to manage the challenges from the congregation and his family that impact his identity-based self-esteem (experience of satisfaction). His identity in Christ is based on Christ and not on how "well" he's pastoring or participating in his family's life. His calling is first and foremost as a Christian. His vocation as a pastor and husband/father reflects his primary identity in Christ. Because his identity is in Christ, the emotional strains, and difficulties of living in a fallen world may be less overwhelming or debilitating. Identity-based resources like DifC may provide Pastor Will with the resources needed to withstand the emotional toll of being a pastor and father/husband.

DifC and Salience

Salience is the second type of resource offered by DifC. Salience refers to the ability to determine which demand is most important at a given time. As emotional, time, and resource demands are made on the pastor from both the congregation and the family, it is difficult to discern which demand is more important at a given time. Salience provides identity-based resources allowing pastors to determine how and where to respond.

Pastors experience a higher risk of burnout when they react to demands from the family and congregation. That is, pastors with performance-based or role-based identities will respond to crises and stress when they arise in unhelpful ways. These types of pastors react and do not respond to the demands of others. These reactions may foster unhealthy relationship patterns in their families and ministries. Gilbert (2006) identifies four emotional processes for anxiety or stress management in families: (1) triangulation, (2) conflict, (3) distance, and (4) over-functioning/under-functioning reciprocity. We see conflict and distance in Pastor Will's relationships with his congregation and family.

Triangulation occurs in relationships when one party draws a third party into a relationship to manage stress. An example of triangulation based on Pastor Will's situation would be for him to include a deacon in his relationship with his wife. He could "consult" or complain to the deacon about how his wife has been treating him recently. He would attempt to get empathy and support from the deacon in order to manage the conflict and stress he's facing with his wife. In fact, one of the challenges Pastor Will is facing is due to how he triangulated Teresa into this relationship with the church. Early in his ministry, he would bring Teresa into his relationship with the congregation during times of stress in order to manage his reaction to the congregation. He would complain to Teresa, and she would take his side. She would empathize with his stress. She would listen to him complain. She felt closer to him during these times. Unfortunately, triangulation only masked the distance and stress in her relationship with Pastor Will. Once the tension and conflict were revealed in their relationship, Pastor Will could no longer rely on Teresa as an ally against the congregation.

The most damaging type of relationship pattern is over-/under-functioning reciprocity. This type of pattern describes how one partner takes over-responsibility for the relationship while the other partner becomes increasingly helpless and irresponsible. In Pastor Will's relationship with Teresa, his complaining to her resulted in her taking responsibility for his emotions. Pastor Will would feel bad and then reach out to process his experiences with Teresa. Teresa would take responsibility to soothe her husband's upset. Teresa ended up neglecting her own emotional needs in the relationship, and she took on a care-taker role for Pastor Will which deprived him of the opportunity to learn how to manage conflict with the congregation (and Teresa) without her help.

These patterns ultimately reflect a reaction to stress and conflict. The individual reacts according to his or her psychological resources to the environment (Friedman, 1985; Hall, 1991). When demands are made from the congregation, the pastor will react to them based on his level of DifC. If he has lower levels of DifC, and his self-esteem is tied into his role as a pastor, he will react in a manner to please the congregation.

Over time, this reaction will spread throughout the congregation, making them reflect the identity of the pastor. In other words, the congregation will take on the personality and identity of the pastor (Friedman, 1985). The pastor's identity may be projected onto the congregation, and over time, the congregation may adopt the same identity and relational style. If the pastor has a strong sense of DifC and embodies this identity in dealing with stress and strain in relationships with both the congregation and the family, they may develop more healthy ways of relating based in their levels of DifC. We see negative examples of this, especially on social media. Often the most confrontational and aggressive Christian social media accounts have pastors (or are pastors) with similar characteristics. When these individuals and pastors experience rebuke from others, there is a tendency to immediately defend against these rebukes. The inability to humbly embrace one's identity and relate with others during differences of opinion reflects lower levels of DifC.

Salience as a DifC resource provides the values-base needed to discern which demands are most important during stressful experiences. If the pastor is basing his identity and self-esteem off his relationships, conflict will demand he comply with the demands of the relationship partner to maintain his sense of identity—I am only a good pastor when I am not in conflict with my flock. The same goes for the family. Demands from both the family and the congregation challenge the limited role-based resources the pastor has to manage these conflicts. DifC anchors the self in Christ. This becomes the values-base to respond to demands from the family and church.

Returning to Pastor Will

In our conversations with Pastor Will, we began identifying how he reacted to his wife and congregation. We highlighted how he would connect with Teresa at times when he was experiencing intense stress in his relationship with Deacon Aaron. Deacon Aaron had been a member of the church for thirty years, and he fancied himself as the holder of the church's history and identity. He was always trying to make sure Pastor Will knew who spoke for the church and did things the "right" way. After deacon meetings, Pastor Will felt deflated and attacked. He would head straight for Teresa to manage his feelings. Pastor Will was under-functioning in his relationship with Deacon Aaron and Teresa. He would not confront the deacon, and he relied on Teresa for emotional regulation. This pattern ultimately depleted his emotional resources as he was relying on his relationships with Teresa and Aaron for his identity as a husband and pastor.

As Pastor Will practiced some of the spiritual disciplines described in chapters 6 and 8, he was able to increase his DifC. The result of this work was his ability to manage his own emotions and engage more directly with Deacon Aaron so that his vision and leadership for the church would be implemented. Salience allowed him to determine how and the best way to respond to both Deacon Aaron and Teresa.

DifC—Differentiation in Christ—provides crucial resources as satisfaction and salience that address the unique context of ministry. The social context of ministry provides a challenge in terms of how the congregation, pastor, and family interact, which often causes pastoral burnout. Often these interactions are ambiguous in nature. Further, calling, especially as defined in terms of our identity in Christ or DifC, addresses the meaningfulness and identity base for doing ministry. Spiritual resources are needed to reinvigorate the pastor and the sense of call. Chapter 6 describes some of these resources.

6

Excursus on Christian Spirituality

Introduction

IN THIS CHAPTER, WE review the concept of Christian spirituality. Some of the main resources to cope with and prevent burnout are spiritual in nature. For some pastors, there is a concern over using traditional Christian spiritual practices or what are known as spiritual disciplines due to the origins of these practices and their similarity to mindfulness. These spiritual disciplines are referred to generally as Christian devotion meditation (CDM). A goal of this chapter is to reclaim Christian devotional practices so that pastors may confidently use them to cope with job stress and burnout. To reconnect these traditional practices with the current church, we will utilize Richard Foster's six streams of spiritual practice. These common streams describe how ancient practices develop an intentional imitation of Christ, which is the goal of Christian spirituality.

This chapter will also focus on:

1. Defining Christian spirituality as the embodiment of Christian beliefs and practices resulting in unity with Christ expressed in vertical and horizontal relationships.
2. Addressing some of the current objections to traditional spiritual disciplines.
3. Describing streams of Christian spiritual disciplines for spiritual practices that are useful for reinvigoration and resources for coping with stress and burnout.

We begin this chapter with a challenging situation. Pastor Mike has been in ministry for over ten years. As we reflect on Pastor Mike, we are reminded of the questions for pastors that Matt Smethurst (2021, loc. 534) mentioned in chapter 3 of *Deacons*:

> How are things going in your church? Is it everything you dreamed it would be? If you're a pastor and you're nodding, I'm guessing it's your second month. Your shirt still bears the faint aroma of a seminary coffee shop. If you're smiling, you're probably in your second year. You reflect on your naïve idealism with a slight eyeroll. If you're crying, you're probably in your second decade. You still have a big ministry dream: it's called a sabbatical.

Pastor Mike is somewhere between idealism and tears. He has seen his church growing and adding members. He has seen some dear friends leave the church due to a nasty split two years ago. One of the members that left is the godparent to Mike's second son. Since that time, Pastor Mike has been under increasing scrutiny as revenues have fallen. He has been providing more pastoral care in terms of visitation and outreach. Further, three deacons left during the split, and he had to take on their tasks. At the same time, Pastor Mike and his wife, Elaine, experienced a miscarriage. Fortunately for Pastor Mike, his church adopted the plurality of elders leadership style, and there are three lay elders assisting with some of the pastoral tasks. One of the elders supports Mike and wants him to focus on his emotional healing by meditating and reading Scripture, relying on practices used throughout church history. The second elder wants Mike to find a good Christian counselor to help with the stressors and grief. The third elder wants Mike to make sure he finds Christian resources to help him and be careful of those "new age" and "Catholic contemplative" practices. How does Pastor Mike decide what to do? Does he call a Christian therapist? Does he rely only on his prayer life with God? We believe in the power of prayer, and God uses his word in power to bring about healing, but are there spiritual practices that Christians shouldn't do? Pastor Mike is unsure of how to proceed.

We approach situations like Pastor Mike's with the understanding that there are valid concerns over different types of spiritual and Christian devotion meditation (CDM) practices. We recommend Christians use CDM practices that fit within their church's and personal theological perspectives. At the same time, we want to offer some encouragement to read more broadly and try different practices as certain practices work better than others for each individual. Having knowledge of the concerns with the various traditions of spiritual practices allows pastors to use these approaches to cope with stress and burnout. Understanding the potential pitfalls and potential benefits aids pastors in developing a toolbox of many different Christian spiritual practices.

Religion and Spirituality

The main concern with certain spiritual practices is thinking about the background and worldview assumptions that are implicit in spiritual and religious strategies that are not explicitly Christian but are still useful for coping with stress and burnout. The worldview framework supporting various spiritual practices may pose concerns for Christians. This chapter is intended to address some of the concerns with various Christian practices throughout church history. Chapter 7 will discuss some concerns with mindfulness-based approaches and offer a Christian alternative.

Doug Oman (2013) describes how religion consists of the organizational and institutional dimensions of faith traditions. Religion provides the worldview content for one's faith. In this sense, religion is the meaning-making and institutional dimensions of faithful practice, belief, and even affect (see Smith, 2009). Religion forms the larger cultural and institutional support needed for individuals to embody their faith, traditions, and practices, including spirituality.

Defining religion as cultural and institutional while defining spirituality as more focused on individual experience and practice emphasizes their distinct aspects yet describes their important interrelationships. Religion encompasses one's faith tradition and community meaning-making aspects of "searching for the sacred" (Pargament, 1992, p. 204), while spirituality focuses on the individual's specific actions and beliefs. In this manner, spirituality is the individual's expression and experience of religion. In other words, *spirituality is the personalized embodiment of one's religion.*

In thinking about spirituality as embodied religion, we are emphasizing the contribution of doctrine and worldview for how individuals live out their faith commitments. The individual learns about the larger meaning of the religion and how this religion makes sense of the world in which the person lives. Further, religion provides liturgical resources for life. These resources inform daily practices based on the doctrines of religion. These daily practices instill a sense of the sacred in everyday life.

Aspects of Christian Spiritual Traditions

Christian spirituality is often conceived of as life "lived under the direction and power of the Holy Spirit" (Demarest, 2012, p. 17). The focus for Christians is becoming more and more like Christ. Christian spiritual practices should result in the person—inside and out—looking increasingly like the Savior. Submission to Christ is paramount to reflecting Christlikeness (1 John 2:3–7). Christian spiritual practices foster an inner conformity to Christ, and these practices encourage us to act more like Christ.

As will be discussed, there are two central facets of Christian spirituality—the apophatic (wordless silence) and the cataphatic (word-based). Both of these components are helpful for pastors to consider. Authentic Christian spiritual disciplines incorporate both aspects (silence and word), for enflaming the heart, feeding the head, and motivating action to foster Christlikeness. Grounding contemplative practices in the word, combined with intentional focus on good theology, fosters a heart transformation needed to persevere through the experience of depletion when the pastor experiences burnout.

There are two main approaches to classify Christian spiritual practices (Demarest, 2012). First, there is an *apophatic* way that steers clear of words and images in order to apprehend the God who is beyond words. This is a "word-less" method for approaching spiritual practices intended to experience God without the burden of human speech. These approaches foster an inner silence intended to allow a spiritual intimacy with God that happens outside the negative biases of word and perspective.

In this approach, words project the person's biases and experiences onto the God who is entirely other and beyond human knowledge. Apophatic approaches see God as totally other and beyond description. Due to the limitation of human speech to capture the otherness of God, words are intentionally abstained from in prayer and other spiritual practices. Silence is emphasized allowing the practitioner to experience God on God's terms, not human ones. One of the best examples of Christian literature in this approach is *The Cloud of the Unknowing* by an anonymous author from the fourteenth century. Centering prayer as developed and practiced by Keating (2014) and Blanton (2011, 2021) is another popular apophatic method. We will have more to say about centering prayer in chapter 8.

One of the main concerns with apophatic approaches concerns the view of God implied in these types of spiritual practices. Coe (2019) identifies the worldview concerns with some forms of apophatic approaches to spirituality. Namely, these approaches tend to identify God with creation, which is known as pantheism. God in this view is creation, and the practitioner needs to empty him or herself and contemplate creation in order to catch and experience unity with God. Unity with God here is a loss of distinction between the Creator and the creature. Individuals practicing these approaches gain enlightenment by apprehending the god within or perceiving the connections between the self and ultimate reality within. In other words, individuals experience spiritual growth to the level they understand that God is within them and that they are ultimately part of the world.

One implication of this is seeing a high degree of similarity and affinity of the human soul with the God who is spirit. The human soul contains or has some God-like qualities so that emptying the self is unifying with God. The focus of this type of wordless contemplation entails eschewing attachment to the material and allowing God, who is spiritually in us, to reveal himself to us wordlessly. The goal of using silence focuses on emptying "consciousness in an attempt to empty the self in order to return to its divine origin" (Coe, 2019, p. 23). Silence allows one to merge with the divine as the view is that the self or soul is partly divine. Words mediate and obscure the connection between the soul and the divine. Words represent attachment to the changing and corrupted physical realm. They ultimately distance or remove one's connection with the creation and creator. Abstaining from words allows for the merging of the self and the divine. This view of God is a concern with mindfulness approaches and certain forms of contemplative prayer like centering prayer. However, we will present a Christian corrective to these concerns below and in chapters 7 and 8.

These are significant concerns for Christians using apophatic approaches to spirituality. John Coe (2019) grounds Christian contemplation, as opposed to meditation and contemplation, in the ontological distinction between the Creator and creature. First, no one can know God unless God reveals his nature. As creatures being made in his image, humanity has the capacity to recognize this divine revelation. Knowledge of God is dependent on revelation, not human activity, or attainment. Second, one's personal knowledge of God is constituted by Christ's work on the cross. That is, through being reconciled to God by Christ's saving work, humanity has the opportunity to know God as savior and not only as judge. Finally, personal knowledge of God develops through the empowerment of the Holy Spirit. The Holy Spirit enlivens the human spirit and empowers humanity to know God and be conformed to the image of his Son, Jesus.

John Coe then defines Christian contemplation and contemplative prayer this way:

> Contemplation (contemplative prayer) is the act and experience whereby our human spirit opens to and attends to the indwelling Spirit of Christ, who is continually revealing himself to us and bearing witness to our spirit that we are children of God, loved by Christ, but in such a way that this opening of our spirit is in fact due to the movement of God's Spirit by which we even cry out to God—"Abba, Father"—in the first place. (2019, p. 31)

Locating contemplation clearly in God's work and Word (Jesus Christ) provides a corrective to the dangers in apophatic approaches. Losing the Word in this spiritual discipline entails a loss of distinctions between the self and other, the self and nature, the self and God. Coe's approach to contemplation captures the benefit of attending to the Other who is beyond everything by focusing on Christ and the Spirit. Revelation or knowledge obtained in contemplation is based on communion with God via Christ in the power of the Spirit. This revelation is about the self and how it reflects (or fails to reflect) Christ. Revelation here pushes us towards increased Christlikeness or increased union with Christ as the perfect image of God in human form.

The second approach is word oriented. Cataphatic approaches entail those aspects of Christian spirituality focused on Bible reading and meditation fostering an understanding of God based on his word. Whitney (2014) describes the following cataphatic types of spiritual disciplines: Bible intake, prayer, worship, evangelism, service, stewardship, fasting, silence and solitude, journaling, and learning. To begin with, Whitney lists personal Christian practices that foster holiness inside and out. Further, we can see silence as part of this list. Silence for Whitney is about removing oneself from conversation partners and focusing on one's inner life with God. Sometimes this silence and solitude is wordless; however, these times of silence are focused on relationships with people, not God. Further, these practices are derived from the word of God—the Bible. The other disciplines are centrally word oriented in that they occur in communities which require communication. Whitney (2014, p. 235) describes this well:

> What we are when we are alone is what we really are. If we habitually seek God and His perspective through His Word when we are alone—and not just at church or when with other Christians—then we may be hopeful that we do know God.

Having silent alone time with God allows us to learn who we are and who we are in God. Whitney (2014) is making the point that even in our "silent" practices, we are communing with God. In this silent commune with God, we are sharing and waiting for God's spirit to reveal himself to us and to continue transforming us into the perfect likeness of his Son.

One of the dangers of only using cataphatic approaches to spirituality entails more head knowledge as opposed to heart knowledge. Practicing word-based spirituality—reading the Bible, preaching, and worship—emphasizes knowing God cognitively. A central aspect of Christian spiritual practices is having both head and heart knowledge of God that results in increasing Christlikeness (Foster, 1998, 2011). The concern here is emphasizing doctrine over experience.

Christian spirituality combines both apophatic (wordless, silence) and cataphatic (word oriented) approaches to spirituality. Both these paths lead to the transformation of the person from the inside out. Reflecting on Christian spirituality necessitates a concerted effort to incorporate *contemplation and action* into lived Christian experience. The connection between Christian belief and practice—between doctrine and personal holiness—focuses on Christian spiritual practices often described as spiritual disciplines. The overarching goal or purpose of spiritual disciplines is developing Christlikeness (Whitney, 2014). The Christian component of the disciplines describes the outcome and is embedded in Christian practices described in both the Bible and in church

Excursus on Christian Spirituality

history. In other words, Christian spiritual practices are tied into specific Christian beliefs and doctrines (Whitney, 2014) and are needed for achieving *Christlikeness* or what is sometimes called holiness (see Heb 12:14).

The goal of practicing Christian spiritual disciplines is to become more like Christ. Foster (1998) describes the *telos* or purpose of Christian spirituality as an intentional imitation of Christ or *imitatio Christi* in Latin. The emphasis of the spiritual component of Christian spirituality focuses on embodying the behavior as well as transforming the heart of the believer in preparation for unity with Christ. Spirituality here focuses on the inner motivations and experiences of being a Christian. Christians learn to feel like Christ—be angry at the same things, have compassion on others, be zealous for the things of God, etc. On top of this inner unity with Christ, Christians begin to behave as Christ—visiting those in jail, being involved in addressing oppression, and walking alongside those suffering. These spiritual practices culminate in an outward expression of Christianity in treating others as oneself (Matt 7:12).

Christlikeness in this sense has a recursive or circular process. First, we are unified with Christ in his life and death (see Nelson, 2023). This union with Christ means God no longer sees us and our sin, God sees Christ's holy life in place of ours. In the beginning of our movement towards God, his grace in Christ covers us and makes forgiveness and reconciliation possible. After we are born again or regenerated, our motivation is to increasingly become like Christ from the inside out. Our hearts are regenerated by the power of the Spirit, and part of this transformation reorients our feelings away from sin and towards the things of Christ.

We define Christian spirituality, therefore, as *the embodiment of Christian beliefs and practices resulting in unity with Christ expressed in vertical and horizontal relationships*. The focus for our definition is on incorporating both the biblical and Christian tradition as the overarching framework for one's spiritual practices. Following Horton (2013) and Whitney (2014), the drama of Scripture informs our understanding of doctrine (theology proper and distinctive dogmas). Scripture and doctrine provide the beliefs and meaning-making framework (worldview) that is filled with distinctly Christian content. The foundation in Scripture supersedes and corrects errors in doctrine and dogma (Whitney, 2014); however, Christians should retrieve spiritual practices used throughout church history to aid in developing Christlikeness as long as these practices are supported in Scripture.

Six Christian Spiritual Frameworks from Church History

Richard Foster describes six streams of spiritual life that may inform how we become more Christlike. These streams provide general frameworks allowing us to incorporate both the head and the heart to foster an initial development of Christlikeness. In other words, combining all these streams into one's regular Christian spiritual life develops the entire person—inner and outer—to be more like Christ. The first tradition deals with the contemplative life. "The contemplative life is the steady gaze of the soul upon the God who loves us" (Foster, 1998, p. 49). The contemplative life longs for a deeper experience of God's love. Through prayer, the contemplative one develops a sense of God's abiding presence. The emphasis is upon the individual and his or her experience with God. The focus in this stream is the heart.

Contemplative practices include solitude, praying the Scripture, and rest. Solitude as a practice allows us to focus on listening intently to others. Foster (1998) recommends taking an early morning walk to listen to the soundtrack of dawn; he also recommends limiting one's speech and instead focusing on listening to others. Finally, solitude could be found in observing crowds at the mall. The intent is to learn to listen and not speak so that one can hear God.

Praying the Scripture involves "turn[ing] our heart and mind and spirit ever so gently to the divine Center" (Foster, 1998, p. 57). In praying the Scripture, we read and reflect on the word of God and allow it to illuminate us. In this practice, we submit ourselves to the word of God, and we wait to experience the power of the word devotionally.

Rest is the final practice we want to mention. Rest and leisure allow us to rest in God's grace and mercy. Resting is our conscious decision to wait for God's providence and provision. We wait on God to work in our lives. Rest and leisure intentionally challenge us to rely on God's strength for success and not our own.

One of the main concerns with the contemplative approach to Christian spirituality focuses on its otherworldliness. That is, contemplation sometimes results in preoccupation with an inner turn that moves the person away from the world. This inner turn culminates in seclusion or removal from the world—sequestering the self away from attachment to the world.

All the concerns with apophatic approaches are connected here. Contemplation usually involves a wordless movement that is a concern. Incorporating Coe's insights is a step in the right direction.

The second stream in Foster's (1998) view is the holiness tradition. The focus here is on acting rightly and behaving like Christ. The holiness tradition is concerned with living a holy life in the world, as opposed to a spiritual life separate from the world. "The goal of the Christian life is not simply to get us into heaven, but to get heaven into us" (Foster, 1998, p. 85). The holiness tradition deals with developing a redemptive, Christian response to a fallen, sinful world. Christians know when they enter the kingdom by the fruits they display. Being a Christian means embodying holy habits (Matt 7:16). The focus here is on the hand, not the head or heart.

There are three main components of spiritual practices in the holiness tradition. First, there is an emphasis on training. The focus in training is doing things to build up our spiritual muscles. We rely on this tradition to develop, to do things to discipline the body and spirit, to cultivate the fruit of the Spirit. Second, there is a focus on spiritual companionship. We find mentors and companions to aid us in the journey and provide a sense of accountability. Third, when we invariably fall, we get back up and begin again. The core metaphor here is athletics. We train the body with the help of spiritual friends. When setbacks happen, we resume the path of training.

The focus on personal ethics and action in the holiness stream tends to become a behavioral system devaluing the Spirit-filled, inner life. In emphasizing the behavioral and ethical, there is a tendency towards legalism (Foster, 1998). This penchant for legalism emphasizes traditions and practices which are more culture bound or denominational in nature than located in virtues associated with Christianity. Disciples here tend to be caught in doing things (like Martha) which do not count towards righteousness. Conformity to the standard is more important than the condition of the heart.

The charismatic tradition values the Christian's experience with the power of the Holy Spirit. There is a "threefold function of the charisms of the Spirit: leadership, ecstatic empowerment, and community-building" (Foster, 1998, p. 126). Discipleship and spirituality in the charismatic tradition tend towards a spiritual warfare metaphor. There is an emphasis on equipping and exercising supernatural gifts like healing, speaking in tongues, and exorcism. The concern here is the experience of the Holy Spirit in the life of the believer (Foster, 1998). Disciples should see the immanent or realized kingdom of God in the present. The Spirit comes with power to the life of the believer now. This tradition fosters attention towards "life in and through the Spirit of God" (Foster, 1998, p. 125). The focus here is on power and spirit, not head or heart.

In general, specific charismatic practices involve connecting with the Spirit. First, it may be helpful to connect with trusted mentors and friends that are more familiar with these practices. Maybe attend a more Pentecostal or charismatic church service. Second, foster a teachable spirit. Lean in to where God's Spirit is working on you. Step out in faith. If you feel prompted to pray for someone, do so. If the Spirit is moving you to reach out in conversation with someone, do so. As Foster encourages us, "step out confidently knowing that God is with you and will be your strength" (1998, p.

132). The final recommendation is to test your spiritual leanings with the word of God and trusted spiritual mentors.

Foster (1998) identifies several concerns with the charismatic approach to spiritual disciplines. First, there is a tendency towards replacing the gift with the Giver. Disciples often seek after the manifestation of the gift rather than the Giver of the gift. This tendency is sometimes expressed in emphasizing the gifts of the Spirit from the fruit of the Spirit—power over character. Another set of concerns is related to having a more anti-intellectual and anti-theological approach tied into one that is more experiential. Additionally, there is a tendency towards end-times prophecy and speculation regarding the second coming of Christ.

The next stream of the Christian spiritual life concerns social justice. The central concern of this stream is "justice and shalom in all human relationships and social structures" (Foster, 1998, p. 137). In this approach, the personal desire for holiness is expressed to community, neighborhood, and society. The righteous or holy person seeks to extend this holiness throughout society, so God's justice and righteous way of living characterizes culture. Social and cultural transformation is the goal here, not the heart or mind of the individual.

Foster (1998) suggests that the first step in the social justice stream is education. That is, we should recognize that (1) God uses "ordinary" Christians to make a difference in the lives of others. Further (2) a crucial step is to learn about those in need, learn about the powerless and exploited, and then (3) advocate for them. Finally (4) we can support agencies and organizations that support the powerless by giving money, volunteering, and prayer.

The concern in the social justice tradition focuses on the goal of this approach. Foster (1998) describes how the social justice view could become the central feature divorced from a biblical view of God's justice and shalom. One of the tendencies in the social justice tradition is replacing biblical notions of justice with social ones. When this happens God's kingdom is viewed as a potentially achieved utopia based on prevalent cultural notions of justice. Developing a good, just society can become the goal or *telos* of society instead of having a redeemed creation that will glorify God. Another potential weakness of the social justice tradition is the potential that justice becomes laws and regulations like the Pharisees. The final weakness occurs when the social justice tradition of the church becomes identified with a particular political agenda so that the church can no longer critique the political agenda.

The fifth tradition of the Christian church is the evangelical tradition which "focuses upon the proclamation of the evangel, the good news of the gospel" (Foster, 1998, p. 187). The central focus of the evangelical tradition is Jesus Christ and his life described in the Bible. This approach is centrally word focused. The primary spiritual focus in the evangelical tradition is Christocentric, focusing upon right Christology. The tendency of the evangelical tradition is to separate from the world because of proper doctrine. Evangelicals may separate from mainline denominations based upon the search for the right doctrine. There is also a tendency to limit the multilayered meanings of Christ's death and resurrection, which leads to a "bibliolatry" (Foster, 1998, p. 230). The tendency is to focus upon the Scriptures so that they take precedence even over Christ. In this tradition, the head is emphasized over the heart.

There are two main dimensions of evangelical spirituality according to Foster (1998). First, we need to focus on the gospel. This means spending time in the word—both Testaments. The more we know about the Bible and how it transforms us, the better. The second dimension of evangelical spirituality is knowing our neighbors. We preach the gospel of Christ by paying attention to our neighbors and living out our Christ callings in their midst.

Some of the concerns of the evangelical tradition are associated with *biblicism*. This happens when the Bible itself becomes an idol. There is a tendency of the evangelical tradition to separate because of proper doctrine—splitting over secondary and lower doctrines. Evangelicals may separate from mainline denominations based upon the search for the right doctrine.

The final tradition is the incarnational tradition. The incarnational tradition centers upon the embodied expression of Christ

Excursus on Christian Spirituality

through the Spirit. The central focus is the church's life together glorifying God in the world (Foster, 1998). The sacraments become the most visible forms in the life of the church that demonstrate the invisible God becoming visible in his Son. "Sacraments are concrete actions by which we are marked and fed in such a way that the reality of God becomes embedded in our body, our mind, our spirit" (Foster, 1998, p. 262). Spirituality and spiritual disciplines in the incarnational tradition are realized in the material expression of the world. The focus here is knowledge and action as mediated by the church as opposed to the transformation of the heart.

The first step into incarnational spirituality is invocation. We invite the Spirit of God to invigorate all reality—our jobs, our experiences. We invite God to make his presence known to us. Second, we need to recapture a sacred understanding of our work—vocation or calling—especially as pastors. God called you to minister to his flock. In the day to day of ministry, it is easy to lose sight of the sacred dimension of pastoring. Third, we should live covenantally. Our marriages and commitments reflect God's covenantal nature, and they provide an opportunity to live out our covenantal commitments before God.

Foster (1998) describes two central concerns of the incarnational approach. First, idolatry is a major concern. In other words, there is danger in this tradition to merge the sacred object with the spiritual reality behind the object (Foster, 1998, p. 267). There is a tendency to see God's splendor replete throughout the creation, and the church, then, is the most accurate representation of that splendor expressed in liturgy. As a result, the church may worship the culture as the physical expression of Christ, even when culture is evil and anathema. Disciples in this tradition may equate God with creation as opposed to God being above creation. The second concern focuses on how liturgy and sacrament could be an attempt to control God. The incarnational, sacramental view could rely on its liturgy to contain God or limit his action or power in the world. This would limit one's spiritual connection to the liturgy prescribed by the incarnational church.

Implications for Pastors Struggling with Burnout

Pastors would benefit from recalling the two central aspects of Christian spirituality—the apophatic (wordless silence) and the cataphatic (word-based). Authentic Christian spiritual disciplines incorporate both aspects (silence and word), heart, head, and action to foster Christlikeness. Grounding contemplative practices in the word, combined with intentional focus on good theology, fosters a heart transformation needed to combat the ravages of burnout as a pastor. As we revisit our earlier example with Pastor Mike, we encourage anyone in his situation to (1) look into spiritual practices connected with his or her church tradition and (2) incorporate one or two practices to start with. As burnout does not happen overnight, it is important to have patience and take your time to work on the practices that are most meaningful to you. We will offer three specific Christian spiritual practices in chapter 8 as well as develop a personal plan to cope with pastoral burnout in chapter 9.

7

Christian Mindfulness Approaches to Managing Burnout in the Pastorate

Introduction

CHAPTER 7 WILL DESCRIBE some of the research on mindfulness approaches to coping with burnout. The focus here will be on identifying specific practices for pastors to use. Some of these practices are useful for in-the-moment coping strategies. Other strategies are useful long-term practices that foster deeper emotion regulation.

Mindfulness

In this chapter we will review some of the literature on mindfulness and its benefits, describe the concept of Christian mindfulness, and move into practices utilizing Christian mindfulness to cope with stress and burnout demands associated with ministry. "Mindfulness can be thought of as moment-to-moment, nonjudgmental awareness, cultivated by paying attention in a specific way, that is, in the present moment, and as non-reactively, as non-judgmentally, and as openheartedly as possible" (Kabat-Zinn, 2015, p. 1481). In other words, mindfulness is a characteristic of mental states that emphasizes observing and attending to our current experiences as well as our thoughts and emotions (Hill & Updegraff, 2012). We can think of mindfulness as a way of intentionally and purposefully paying attention to our experience. The practice of mindfulness has become part of the burnout conversation. In the past four decades, the concept of mindfulness has received extensive attention within the discipline of psychology. Mindfulness approaches began with stress reduction in the 1970s and 1980s. Since that time, many clinicians have incorporated mindfulness practices as part of their treatment plans (Hülsheger et al., 2013).

Mindfulness enhances work-related outcomes such as task performance, increases job satisfaction, and positively influences attitudes and behaviors (Dane, 2011; Glomb et al., 2011; Hülsheger et al., 2013). Research also shows that mindfulness has been effective in treating multiple ailments. For example, mindfulness has been shown to reduce stress, anxiety, rumination, and mood disorders (Hawley et al., 2014; Troy et al., 2013). Mindfulness has also been used to treat substance use disorders and addiction (Lee Lloyd Johnson, 2019). Depression has also been successfully treated with mindfulness (Rigas et al., 2022). A study by Lee and Jang (2021) found that mindfulness can enhance positive emotions and reduce negative emotions. From a physical standpoint, mindfulness has been shown to alter cortisol and immune levels, which is associated with reduced stress levels and mood disturbances, and decreased blood pressure (Carlson et al., 2007). Mindfulness can reduce the impact of headaches, but not the frequency of headaches (Hunt et al., 2023). These studies show that mindfulness can produce positive outcomes for a number of conditions, but what about stress and burnout?

As discussed in chapter 2, burnout comprises exhaustion, cynicism, and inefficacy. These three dimensions are a response to chronic emotional and interpersonal stressors (Maslach et al.,

2001). Hester (2017) defines pastoral burnout as unaddressed stress attributed to ministry that without proper management evolves into chronic emotional fatigue, isolation, apathy, and an inability to recognize one's own accomplishments. Pastors often suffer in silence and, while they are often seen as the problem solver for their congregants, they may be alienated from the peace of Christ. Burnout can manifest as irritability, exhaustion, depression, or suicidal ideation. Burnout can lead to job/role turnover as well as mental health issues (Trammel & Trent, 2021). As we discussed in chapter 3, individuals who work in service jobs, particularly helping roles (such as the pastorate) are confronted with emotional labor (Hochschild, 1983, 2012). As such, they have to attend to emotional display rules that are prescribed by the work role, occupation, or organization that govern the expression of emotions (Rafaeli & Sutton, 1987) and are more likely to experience stress and burnout as a result. In other words, the requirements of service jobs can become a job hazard for employees who work in these fields.

For pastors who are seeking help, mindfulness has been proven to effectively treat stress and burnout. The vast majority of research shows mindfulness, when practiced regularly, can help reduce burnout and the consequences of job-related burnout. Job demands and resources (JD-R) predict burnout. Have you experienced high work demands and/or lack of resources you needed to complete your work? High demands and low resources can lead to stress and burnout. Mindfulness moderates the effects of job demands and job resources (Zhang et al., 2022). In other words, mindfulness can help employees cope with high demands and low resources. Mindfulness has also been shown to maximize neurological connections in the brain that support emotional regulation which helps to decrease reactivity. Other studies have found that mindfulness can improve compassion, reduce burnout, increase self-compassion, reduce psychological symptoms, reduce stress, and increase sense of well-being (Flook et al., 2013; McNulty et al., 2022; Nguyen et al., 2020; van der Riet et al., 2018). Studies have also found that, for employees working in emotionally demanding jobs, mindfulness promotes job satisfaction and helps prevent burnout in terms of emotional exhaustion (Hülsheger et al., 2013). Specifically related to pastoring, Moceri and Cox (2019) found that Christian clergy who participated in mindfulness interventions reported a reduction in blood pressure readings and stress levels. Taken together, the empirical evidence demonstrates that mindfulness is a fruitful way to deal with emotional job demands.

Christian Mindfulness

Unlike the secular view of mindfulness, Christian mindfulness includes the active presence of God. In other words, we are paying attention on purpose (mindfulness) by attending to God's presence in our experience. According to Trammel and Trent (2021), it can be thought of as making time to turn our whole attention to God so that we can hear and abide in his voice above the chatter and stress of our lives. It involves activating our awareness toward God's presence through God's word, the Holy Spirit, prayer and even turning our thoughts toward him. The distinction with secular mindfulness is that in Christian mindfulness, we choose to invite Christ into our mind and attention. Mindfulness for Christians is about paying attention to the present moment with Christ as the center of each moment. By practicing mindfulness, we can stay more present with the people we are spending time with or serving. We can better tolerate emotional upheavals. We can improve our listening and communication. We can become better stewards of our time and attention. In short, we can experience God's healing, provision, hope, and restoration more fully physically, mentally, and spiritually (Trammel & Trent, 2021).

Basic Mindfulness Steps

Before moving forward to using practical mindfulness techniques, it is important to first outline the basic steps of mindfulness. Trammel and Trent (2021) provide four basic steps that are universal, which we will build on with additional details and examples. As you review these steps, consider trying each step yourself. Mindfulness techniques can be practiced daily, can be done anywhere, and best of all are not time consuming. Research indicates that engaging in mindfulness while outdoors is especially beneficial.

To begin, the first step of practicing mindfulness is to lower your heart rate and settle your thoughts through breath work. You begin practicing Christian mindfulness by attending to your breath. Breathing is one of the most basic human functions, and it is connected with the spirit (see chapter 8). Focusing on breath allows you to practice paying attention. The physical act of breathing allows you to center your thoughts on the body. You can do this while standing, but a better option is to sit or even lie down comfortably. Your eyes may be open or closed. Notice where you feel the breath in your body. Is it your chest? Your abdomen? Your throat or nostrils? Your thoughts might begin to wander, but try to focus your attention on your breath, then inhale and exhale. The point is to focus on the rhythm of your breathing and allow the calming effect to take over. Stay here for five to seven minutes and notice your breath, in silence. When trying to calm yourself in a stressful moment, it might help to take an exaggerated breath. Try inhaling through your nostrils for a few seconds, hold your breath for two seconds, and exhale through your mouth for four seconds. As you pay attention to your breathing and notice your environment, you can receive these gifts and blessings that God has provided.

The second step of practicing mindfulness is to observe your thoughts and body responses. Think about this step as observing your thoughts from a distance with more objectivity and bringing your thoughts back to the sensations of your body and mind. When practicing mindfulness, your thoughts may wander away from the present moment. Part of mindfulness is noticing when this happens, and then gently resuming the practice. Focusing on the five senses allows us to pay attention to our bodies and our experience. Begin by observing with your five senses. What do you see around you? Watch who and what go by in front of you. Notice the facial expression and movements of another person. Stop for a moment and just listen. If someone is talking, listen to the pitch of the voice, to the pauses between the words, or the inflections they use. What do you smell? Does it linger? Pay attention to the taste in your mouth. Pay attention to anything touching you or in turn touch something and notice the sensations in your hands. Next, observe the thoughts coming in and out of your mind. Ask, Where do these thoughts come from? How do we react? How can we make corrections? When we are engaging in observation, it is critical that we are fully present in the moment. Consider your physical reactions as well as your thoughts and feelings. Begin to turn outward and observe others, how they react to us, how responsible we are for other's feelings and actions, and where our boundaries with them should lie. Using mindfulness techniques such as observation allows us to relate better not only to ourselves, but also with others. Practices like this center us in our bodies; it centers us in our experience so we can see where God is at work in our lives.

The third step of practicing mindfulness is to identify personal values. By values, we mean personal qualities and ways of living you resonate with. A value is not merely a goal, but can be thought of as a continuous process or way of living that helps directs us toward goals we may have to live a meaningful life. This step is critical as it helps to synthesize our observations with our Christian values; it is where we align our thoughts, behaviors, motivations, and temptations with values based on Scripture (Trammel & Trent, 2021).

In the hustle and bustle of daily life, it is easy to lose track of what we truly care about and value. We begin to react in a mindless manner to the stress and strain of daily life. We tend to lose sight of our identities, to respond to others as we intend to. Identifying our values and then paying particular attention to our experiences allows us to live a values-based life. To identify and name your values, begin by taking some time to reflect deeply on which areas of your life and ways of living give you the most meaning, interest, and/or sense of fulfillment. After doing so, evaluate how important each one is to you and rank them in a hierarchical fashion. Next, closely and honestly consider how this value is manifested in your current life including daily activities, lifestyle, and relationships. Make note of any values that you have ranked highly but are not highly present in your life. Next, brainstorm and list any concrete ways you can make this value more present in your life. For example, if you value quality time with your family, perhaps making an effort to have dinner together at least three to four times a week is an actionable change. Finally, continue to think of different ways you can further incorporate your values into your life and test them out. Be sure to take note of what works and what doesn't and, above all, give yourself grace in the process. Identifying and working to further incorporate personal values into our lives can not only add a sense of fulfillment to our lives, but also deepen our sense of purpose and meaning.

The fourth step of practicing mindfulness is to rehearse our responses. One of the most important lessons mindfulness teaches us is to respond to situations rather than react. Reacting typically occurs quickly and without thought—in a mindless manner. It can happen in moments of anger, frustration, or even annoyance. A response, however, is typically well thought out, calm, and compassionate. Rehearsing a right way to act is part of a general mindfulness contemplation (Trammel & Trent, 2021). Rehearsal of thoughts and planned action helps us to recognize the types of thoughts we are having and the awareness of what is most honest and true about our situation while in the present moment. Rehearsing means we are staying in the moment, staying aware, and trying to expand our compassion for ourselves and others. It is where we make a conscious, meaningful decision after taking time to observe the situation and think. Mindfulness helps us to notice the space before we react and instead cultivate the ability to self-regulate and respond in healthier ways. When we are able to build this awareness, we begin to recognize our mental or emotional habits and set new intentions for ourselves. To practice this step, try to recognize the way you feel or the thoughts you are having more often as they arise. In situations, refrain for a moment from doing whatever you typically do. Pause and take a few breaths, and let things alone before taking a next step. Try to relax (if you can) and let go of any sense of tension. Resolve to keep working on rehearsing your responses rather than being reactive. For pastors, this step is a wonderful opportunity to rehearse those things that are beyond us and often are where we find ourselves depending on Christ. We rehearse understanding his will, the Holy Spirit's guidance, the Scripture that makes the truth clear to us (Trammel & Trent, 2021).

Additional Mindfulness Practices

Now that you are familiar with the basic steps of mindfulness, we are ready to explore different strategies. That is, the four general practices discussed above are foundational to the following practices. Each of the following practices is based on the four principles described above. Keep in mind that these strategies are not a one size fits all. You may find that some are more appealing or simply doable for you than for others. There is also no set number of strategies or techniques you must implement to benefit from the practice. Challenge yourself to practice some form of it daily for six months. You may find that after this period of time, it will become effortless and as a result you may respond more effectively to stress and other negative internal experiences. Studies also show mindfulness practices can build individual leadership capacity and effectiveness (Lange and Rowold, 2019). Let's get started on some exercises you can try starting today.

Journaling

Journaling is an inexpensive and portable way to engage in mindfulness. In essence, it helps us to make sense of our thoughts, feelings, perspectives and increase our understanding as it happens. Writing is a very focused action, is slower than thinking, and requires our full attention. While the type of journal you use is personal preference (e.g., plain, digital, app based), research indicates physical writing (if possible) is better at creating the mindfulness experience as it enforces retention and limits distraction more than typing on a computer or device. The physical act to thinking about what we are writing fosters our attention for a purpose. Journaling allows us to shift through our experiences and intentionally write about them. Putting aside ten minutes a day to focus on journaling can help you manage anxiety, reduce stress, and improve your mental health. You may be wondering, Okay, but how do I start? Mindfulness journals often have specific prompts to follow. This is intentional as the questions are typically designed to elicit self-awareness. Trammel and Trent (2021) provide helpful prompts for pastors:

- What are your congregation's most pressing needs? What is your role in meeting those needs?
- How good are you at meeting your spiritual, mental, emotional, and physical needs? What needs are you neglecting? What needs are you meeting?
- How would you describe your sense of God's presence in your life? Name three to five ways God's presence is working through you.
- Name three people in your life you are thankful for and explain why. Name three people you need to lean on more.

Journaling does not have to be limited to writing. You can get creative and doodle or, if you are more artistic, express yourself in a creative way. The most important thing is that you make the journal your own, do what works for you, and do what you find easiest to stick to. If you are not interested in prompts, opt to write in your journal daily. Writing in the evening and reflecting on your experiences, responses, thoughts, and feelings of the day is a helpful way to decompress.

Caring for Our Shepherds

Eating, Sleeping, and Walking

Mindfulness extends to our eating, sleeping, and exercise habits as well. How many of us reach for unhealthy snacks when stressed or to eat altogether? Eating mindfully refers to being intentional about the foods being chosen, internal and external physical cues, and your responses to those cues. It is a practice to slow down the experience by contemplating, savoring, and being grateful for the blessing of food rather than wolfing it down in order to get to the next task, as many do in this busy day and age.

> You may recall that Shadrach, Meschach, and Abednego set themselves apart from others in the royal Babylonian court by consuming vegetables and water instead of the rich foods and wine served regularly. They asked the guard of the court to test their health after ten days to compare it with the health of other members of the royal court. These three believers knew that their diet not only was healthier for them but also was a demonstration of their identity as followers of Yahweh, the God of Abraham, Isaac, and Jacob. And God blessed their choice. (Trammel & Trent, 2021, p. 147)

By eating mindfully, we are honoring our bodies. Give the following Christian mindful eating practice a try:

- Get rid of distractions by putting your phone down, closing your laptop, or turning off the TV.
- Give thanks for the food and pray a blessing over it.
- Notice how the food looks, tastes, smells, and feels in our bodies as you eat.
- Be intentional about slowing your meal down and listening to your body.
- Acknowledge how your body feels during and after eating.
- Express gratitude once the meal is complete.

Another area of our lives impacted by stress is sleep. When we are overloaded with burdens, it becomes difficult to turn our

Christian Mindfulness Approaches to Managing Burnout

thoughts off at night. This is because stress can cause anxiety and tension, so you may find yourself tossing and turning, waking frequently, or unable to sleep altogether. Sleep is crucial to our well-being because it functions to restore our minds and bodies. According to the National Heart, Lung, and Blood Institute, sleep deficiency is linked to many chronic health problems, including heart disease, high blood pressure, stroke, obesity, and depression. The practice of mindfulness, designed with a focus on sleep, provides an opportunity to create the mental space needed to allow sleep to come back. If you find yourself suffering from sleep related issues, try the following exercise before bedtime:

- Turn off the lights and your phone and lie comfortably.
- Place one hand on your chest, the other on your midsection.
- Breathe in slowly through your nose. The hand on your midsection will rise, while the hand on your chest should stay still. This is known as diaphragmatic breathing.
- Picture your lungs filling with air.
- Breathe out slowly. Repeat ten calm, controlled breaths, using your diaphragm instead of your chest.
- Clear your mind and focus on your breathing. Notice your heartbeat. Feel the bed beneath your body.
- Say a prayer to the Lord, thanking him for rest, and ask to bless you with restoration and the ability to sleep.
- If intrusive thoughts appear, acknowledge them, let them go, and return to your breathing.

Rounding out this section on lifestyle practices includes addressing the importance of physical exercise as a stress reducer. Many of us spend much of our days sitting down in front of computers. In the absence of physical activity, the impact on our body and mind is alarming: muscle loss, weight gain, heart disease, and poor mental health. Therefore, finding a pocket of time to engage in physical exercise can help us in a myriad of ways including neurologically and even spiritually. One way in which we can engage in mindful exercise is through a practice called mindful walking. Mindful walking has been shown to improve our psychological and physiological well being (Tsang et al., 2008). Unlike regular walks, mindful walking centered in Christ gives us the opportunity to focus on God's presence, notice the physical experience of walking, and let go of distractions. We recommend the following walk exercise:

- Find a peaceful location where you can be purposeful in the beginning moments of your practice. This space can be indoors or outdoors, in your backyard, in a park, or any other location that is private.
- Notice how your body feels. Are you tense? Are you relaxed? Are you tired?
- Think about what this time will be used for. Is this a time for walking with God, focusing on his presence, or releasing your worries unto him?
- Begin by taking ten to fifteen slow, deliberate steps. Pause and breathe for however long it feels comfortable and repeat this process again.
- Walk at a slower pace and pay close attention to what your body is doing. Think about lifting your foot, moving your leg forward, placing your foot on the ground, and the way your foot connects with the surface beneath you. Feel your heart beat and listen to your breathing.
- Try and focus your mind on the intention of your walk. Say a short prayer asking God to stay with you during this time.
- If your mind wanders, try and bring your focus back to this experience.
- Say a prayer of thanks when it is over and take stock of any word you received while on the walk or how you felt to be in his presence in this way.

Boundary Keeping

Boundaries are important for our personal well-being and in our relationships. Having healthy boundaries allows us to connect with others, but also to protect ourselves. In pastoral work, boundaries often get blurred as the profession is very relationally oriented. In the words of one pastor, "pastoring is not a business transaction. We walk alongside our flock, we pour into them, and we form relationships with them. We are invested in a very personal way, and when something bad happens or if they decide to leave, the pain is very real for us." Christian mindfulness helps us recognize what things, people, or situations are not good for them (Trammel & Trent, 2021). According to Cloud and Townsend (2017), the laws of boundaries is recognizing that we do not have the power to overcome boundary problems alone. Rather, we can confess, submit to God, and ask him to reveal what we must turn away from. By leaning into God's wisdom, we have the power to walk away from problematic boundaries, to reconcile, and change how we deal with others. So how can we develop better boundaries for better relationships? Try this exercise adopted from Trammel and Trent (2021).

- Start by inhaling deeply for four counts and exhaling for four. Repeat this step two to three times.
- Quiet your mind and invite God to dwell in your mind.
- Picture the relationships in your mind and consider who you want to move forward with and who you may need to let go of.
- As you breathe, focus on one relationship that may need boundary work.
- Use this quiet time to identify your thoughts about this person. Do not try to control the thoughts that come and do not judge those thoughts. Continue breathing in and out and invite God to reveal the truth about these thoughts and about this relationship.

- Receive God's wisdom as you ask in what ways you need to work on your behavior with this person. Is it about letting go? Is it about stepping toward that person?
- Acknowledge any insights you received during this quiet time.
- Close this time out by taking a final deep breath and ask God to help you with this boundary keeping.

Christian mindfulness, intentionally paying attention to how Christ is active in our present experiences, is an important psychological resource for pastors coping with burnout. As pastors practice the four foundational practices—breathing, observing thoughts and bodily experiences, identifying values, and rehearsing responses—more psychological resources are developed for coping with pastoral burnout and stress. Several additional practices were described that could support pastors in developing resources to cope with burnout.

8

Christian Spiritual Practices for Managing Burnout in the Pastorate

Introduction

CHAPTER 8 PRESENTS CHRISTIAN devotion meditation (CDM) practices to cope with pastoral burnout. Three CDM practices—*lectio divina*, the Jesus Prayer, and centering prayer—will be offered to aid in coping with ministerial stress and burnout. Christian devotion meditation (CDM), also known as Christian contemplative practices, are uniquely suited to develop the emotional and spiritual resources pastors need for coping with burnout. Pastors experience spiritual emptiness (what we described as acedia in chapter 2) due to two unique aspects of pastoral life. First, since pastors often work alongside their families in the church while simultaneously serving their congregants, pastors experience inter-role conflict due to the high level of boundary ambiguity between their vocational and family lives. Second, pastors need to rely on their psychological resources to provide for their church members due to the emotional labor required of their positions.

Christian devotion meditation is a broad name for many different Christian spiritual practices (Garzon, 2013). This general understanding of Christian spiritual practices includes things like devotional Bible reading (*lectio divina*), the Jesus Prayer, and other Christian practices like contemplative prayer and centering prayer. We would like to organize these practices into either long-term or short-term categories. We mean, by this, that some practices can be used in the moment to cope with stressful experiences. The Jesus Prayer is one of those in-the-moment, short-term practices that allows us to recapture control of breathing and stay in the moment during stressful interactions and experiences. Daily practice is ideal for getting the most benefit out of short-term practices, but it is not required.

Long-term spiritual practices like meditation, contemplation, and centering prayer are useful in cultivating the spiritual and psychological resources needed to cope with pastoral burnout (Frederick et al., 2021). These practices, like centering prayer, need a longer time to see their benefits; and they need longer times for personal daily use. These types of spiritual practices require twenty to thirty minutes of daily practice. However, these practices provide deep and lasting spiritual reinvigoration. The immediate benefit of these practices is not usually felt until a habit of practicing these devotional tools has been established.

Both types of practices foster an increased spiritual reinvigoration. Burnout, as we have described it, is an intensely spiritual depletion. It involves the loss of your sense of calling, and it is reflected in the experience of *acedia*. That is, not only does pastoral burnout reduce our experience and understanding of God's call to the pastorate, but it also fosters a deep sense of indifference towards the needs of others as well as an emotional depletion and loss of spiritual vigor to shepherd God's sheep. CDM aids us in seeing God at work in our present circumstances, and it allows us to experience him anew in the spirit.

The Jesus Prayer

The Jesus Prayer is an ancient form of meditation. It was used in Eastern Christian spirituality, and it is useful for us today (Talbot, 2013). It can be practiced, in the moment, as a form of Christian mindfulness. The Jesus Prayer is, "Lord Jesus Christ, Son of God, have mercy on me, a sinner" (see Talbot, 2013). Some form of the Jesus Prayer likely emerged in the fourth century as a means of remembering God through repetitive short prayers.

The Jesus Prayer should be coupled with breathing. Talbot (2013) emphasizes the connection between breath and spirit—*Pneuma* in Greek—with the prayer. Pairing this short phrase with the breath develops the ability to pray without ceasing based on an inward focus connecting the Jesus Prayer to how we breathe. "So, from the perspective of praying in the breath or Spirit of God with our spirit, or of praying 'without ceasing,' uniting prayer with our breath works very well" (Talbot, 2013, loc. 129). Tying the breath, spirit, and prayer together allows us to reflect and recognize God in this basic human task. And the Jesus Prayer is an excellent prayer tool allowing us to do that.

Vazquez and Jensen (2020) describe how an inner state of quiet is achieved with the slow and intentional repetition of the Jesus Prayer. The authors recommend controlled breathing while repeating the prayer: "Lord Jesus Christ," inhale, "Son of God," exhale, "have mercy on me," inhale, "a sinner," exhale (Vazquez & Jensen, 2020, p. 66). The way in which we experience and practice the Jesus Prayer has changed by intentionally focusing on the breath; we have turned off autopilot; we are paying attention to both the breath and the words. This allows us to respond to our breathing. We can calm ourselves and recenter our experience so we can respond meaningfully to whatever is making a demand on us. This allows us to be aware of the present and focus on the moment. This short prayer and breathing exercise can be done in the moment, as a short-term practice to lessen feelings of stress and burnout (Frederick et al., 2018).

Suggestions for Practicing the Jesus Prayer

We suggest you set aside ten minutes a day to practice the Jesus Prayer. Developing the habit of intentionally combining breathing with prayer fosters a deep sense of praying without ceasing. By praying without ceasing and focusing on the breath, the Jesus Prayer allows you to focus more directly on God who offers peace and comfort, while gently noticing his active presence in experiences, but not being controlled or overwhelmed by those experiences (Knabb & Vazquez, 2018). Our suggestions for praying this prayer are derived from Talbot's (2013) book on the Jesus Prayer.

Step one: We suggest beginning this practice by sitting comfortably on a chair. Begin focusing on your breath—are you breathing slowly or quickly? Is your breath shallow or deep? How does it feel when the air fills your lungs? What is it like breathing out? Sit in this space focusing on your breathing.

Step two: Next, begin to reflect on the prayer. Recite the words: "Lord Jesus Christ, Son of God, have mercy on me, a sinner." As you are reciting the words, reflect on their meaning. What does "Lord" mean? How is Jesus Christ the Lord? Next, focus on Jesus Christ. Who is Jesus the Christ? What did he do? What does his salvation mean for you? The third phrase is "Son of God." How is Jesus the Christ also the Son of God? How does Jesus's Sonship impact your relationship with God? What does Jesus's Sonship mean for his Lordship? The next word group is "have mercy." How do you experience the mercy of the Lord? Is it similar to the parable of the forgiven servants (Matt 18:23–35)? Where do you see and experience God's mercy? The fifth phrase in this prayer is "me, a sinner." What does your sin do to your relationship with God? How do you feel about your sin? What is the relationship between your sin and God's mercy in Jesus Christ?

Step three: After reflecting on the meaning of the Jesus Prayer, begin to pair the prayer with your breathing. *While pairing the prayer and breathing, don't focus on the meaning or your reflections on the prayer from step two.* On inhaling, repeat the words—"Lord Jesus Christ, Son of God." Focus initially on connecting the inhale with the words. Say them slowly while breathing in. As you inhale, take the words into your being. Fill yourself with the breath and Spirit of God—Lord Jesus Christ, Son of God.

On exhaling, repeat the words—"have mercy on me, a sinner." Breathe out your condemnation, your sin. Acknowledge in the exhale that you renounce the sin. Exhale for the cleansing of your inner self via the breath (spirit) God has given you.

Spend around three to five minutes connecting your breathing with the words. Slowly breathe in with the words "Lord Jesus Christ, Son of God" and exhale on "have mercy on me, a sinner." Slowly breathe in, and slowly breathe out. Inhale and exhale. Pay attention to connecting the words with your breathing.

This entire practice should last around ten minutes. We would recommend beginning a personal journal to track your progress in this practice. Reflect on the impact this prayer has on your breathing: (1) Do you notice it is easier (or more difficult) trying to control your breathing in times of stress? (2) Has the prayer improved your connection with God? (3) Has the prayer helped reduce your in-the-moment experiences of stress? (4) Is your mind less distracted in step two of this practice? In chapter 9, we describe journaling to aid you in developing spiritual resources for coping with pastoral burnout, and this practice is very useful for those in-the-moment times when stress happens. Throughout the day, we recommend checking in on your breathing. If you notice rapid or shallow breathing, take a moment to recapture your breathing with the Jesus Prayer.

Lectio Divina

Lectio divina is an ancient practice for reading the Bible. It is a more formalized way to incorporate Scripture into the mind and heart. Devotional Bible reading is one the most important ways in which we learn the heart of God; the word transforms us as we submit ourselves to it (Wilhoit & Howard, 2012). In this manner, we read the word of God for transformation. We take it in;

we meditate on it; we ask it serious questions; and we allow it to transform our souls.

Lectio divina is concerned with devotionally reading the Bible. We bring all our faculties to bear, especially the imagination, and we interrogate the Scriptures (Foster, 2011). Approaching the Scriptures with imagination allows us to engage in both the heart and head aspects needed for transformation (Foster, 2011; Wilhoit & Howard, 2012). "Lectio divina simply means reading the Bible the way it's supposed to be read—as divine Scripture" (Boersma, 2023, p. 13). That is, we use all our faculties to engage the Holy Scriptures for devotional purposes. Incorporating the imagination, informed by the intellect, under the submission of the inspired word of God (2 Tim 3:16), allows us to be transformed by the renewing of the mind in Scripture (Rom 12:1–2).

Imagination is perhaps the key ingredient of *lectio divina*. In encountering the Bible, we need to be conscious of the historical and authorial intent of the passage we are considering. However, we also need to allow the Spirit to work through our faculties to enliven our response to this word. The word creates images and scenes in our minds through *imagination* (Boersma, 2023). Our imaginations allow us to engage the text providing added insight visually and spatially, and it becomes more meaningful for us *personally* in the encounter. We use our imaginations to enter the text. We can visualize the scene for the Sermon on the Mount (Matt 5–7); we can see Peter and Andrew fishing when Jesus calls them to be disciples (Matt 4:18–22). We can even imagine the smell! Foster (2011, locs. 235–36) reminds us: "God created us with an imagination, and as Lord of all creation he can and does redeem it and use it for the work of the kingdom of God." In other words, God uses our imagination as part of our sanctification. The imagination is a core component of *lectio divina*, and we should use this God-given faculty to enter the Scriptures for our spiritual benefit and transformation.

Suggestions for Practicing *Lectio Divina*

There are four general steps for lectio divina. They are (Boersma, 2023; Wilhoit & Howard, 2012): (1) *Lectio* (reading): An attentive, slow, repetitious recitation of a short passage of Scripture; (2) *Meditatio* (meditation): An effort to understand the passage and apply it to my own life; (3) *Oratio* (prayer): Engaging or talking with God about the passage; (4) *Contemplatio* (contemplation): Allowing myself to be absorbed in the words of God as the Holy Spirit draws me into his presence through Scripture. These steps move us from reading the Scripture to contemplation of it. It is moving through these steps which foster transformation and renewal of the mind by the word. We will provide a step-by-step overview of these steps followed by a sample *lectio*.

Step one: *Lectio* means attentive reading where the individual identifies a specific passage of Scripture and slowly reads the passage. This step entails reading and studying the passage. In *lectio*, we ask questions like: What is happening in this passage? What is the context? Who are the main actors? What does this passage reveal about God? In step one, we suggest reading small sections of Scripture several times, focusing on the meaning and context of the passage.

Step two: Meditatio occurs when we begin to focus and attend to the passage we read. We can think of this as an active component of *lectio divina*. Reciting the passage aloud, reviewing it throughout the day. Meditatio means developing intimate familiarity with the passage. Wilhoit and Howard (2012) offer two images for meditation. First, we need to ruminate on the passage. Let it consume our thoughts. Let it be primary in the mind. Chew on it over and over. Second, we need to gnaw or growl on the passage. That is, we need to fully engage with the passage as much as is possible. This is one place where imagination comes to play. We need to walk with the text; repeat the text; "smell" and come to grips with the text—wrestle with it. In all this, we take the text into our souls.

Step three: The third step focuses on praying the Scriptures back to God. We engage in prayer—communicating with God—based on the text. Perhaps we receive some illumination or conviction from the text; we take that to God. Perhaps we see God in new light, and we respond in praise and prayer! We use the text to communicate with God whose word we are reading.

Step four: Contemplatio completes the four processes of *lectio divina*. In contemplation, we wait on the Lord for a response. That is, reading (*lectio*), *meditatio*, and prayer lead us to be silent before God. We are silent enjoying the presence of the Lord, and we wait for any response from God to what we have been praying, reading, and meditating on.

A *Sample* Lectio Divina

Step one (Read):

A. Begin with a short prayer. Focusing on the breath, pray to God. Ask for illumination. Ask for his presence. Pray: "Dear heavenly Father, as I am seeking you in your word, please send your Spirit to encourage me. Let your Spirit empower me as I meditate on your Scriptures. Speak to me. Illuminate me. Convict me. Let me glorify your name. Amen."

B. After praying this prayer, begin reading the following passage.

   1. Slowly and thoughtfully, read the Scripture passage for the first time. What word or phrase captures your attention and grabs your heart? What does this passage teach you about God? What do you learn about yourself?

C. Psalm 86:1–8:

> Incline your ear, O LORD, and answer me,
>   for I am poor and needy.
> 2 Preserve my life, for I am godly;
>   save your servant, who trusts in you—you are my God.
> 3 Be gracious to me, O Lord,
>   for to you do I cry all the day.

> 4 Gladden the soul of your servant,
>   for to you, O Lord, do I lift up my soul.
> 5 For you, O Lord, are good and forgiving,
>   abounding in steadfast love to all who call upon you.
> 6 Give ear, O LORD, to my prayer;
>   listen to my plea for grace.
> 7 In the day of my trouble I call upon you,
>   for you answer me.
> 8 There is none like you among the gods, O Lord,
>   nor are there any works like yours.

Step two (Meditate):

A. Slowly and prayerfully, read the passage again. What is God saying to you in this passage? Asking you? What feelings are arising within you?

B. Use your imagination: What would it be like if you were the psalmist praying this prayer to God? What circumstances would lead you to pray this prayer to God?

C. Is there a word or phrase that resonates with you? What is God saying to you with that word?

Step three (Pray):

A. Slowly and prayerfully, recite your word or phrase again. Respond to God from your heart. Speak to God of your feelings and insights. Offer these to God.

B. Offer to God anything that you learned about him. Offer to God any confession or guilt over missing the mark as revealed in the passage.

C. Offer to God anything you learned about yourself in this passage. Did the passage lead you to glorify and praise God? Did the passage remind you of something you forgot? Did it convict you of something about your relationships with God and others?

Step four (Contemplate):

A. Consider rereading the passage another time. Sit quietly in God's presence, asking, "What are you saying to me?" Be silent in the space created by the word and meditation. Rest in the knowledge that God is for you. That God loves you. That God reveals himself to us and provides everything we need.

B. Thank God for this time spent in *lectio divina* and for any insights you may have been given concerning the text.

C. Doxology—Sing or say: "Glory be to the Father, and to the Son, and to the Holy Spirit, As it was in the beginning, is now and ever shall be, world without end. Amen."

Lectio Divina Follow-Up

The entire *lectio divina* should last from twenty to thirty minutes. The process should begin slowly. We recommend consistently using the same passage of Scripture for this process. It takes time to meditate on Scripture, and the more familiar the passage is the better. At the beginning of using *lectio*, we recommend journaling after the experience. In the journal, it would be helpful to track your progress. Ask questions like: Have I noticed less distraction during the prayer parts of the *lectio*? Is it easier for me to recall the passage I am meditating on as I gain more experience with the practice? Am I noticing any changes in my relationship with God? Has this practice made a difference with my pastoral burnout? Record any thoughts, feelings, and experiences that you feel prompted to. Return to your journal regularly to review and track progress.

Centering Prayer

Centering prayer is a practice that developed in the mid-twentieth century (Keating, 2014; Wilhoit, 2014). This prayer practice developed with Thomas Keating, who was trying to make Christian mystical spiritual practices more accessible to young people. Centering prayer is his attempt at incorporating the spirituality of the *Cloud of Unknowing* with meditative prayer. The purpose of this practice is fostering listening and receptivity so we can hear and notice God's loving and active presence in our lives (Keating, 2014).

By Keating's (2014) own account, centering prayer is the beginning of the contemplative process. Contemplation ends, usually in heaven, when we meet God and apprehend him in himself. Centering prayer, on the other hand, is a willful assent or surrender to God's loving and active presence in one's experience and heart. In other words, centering prayer is a practice for invigorating the will to actively surrender to God's presence.

This practice develops the attitudes of listening and receptivity for God. Centering prayer fosters an inner assent to God's work in our lives and experiences. In developing this heart surrender, practitioners learn to become listeners. They attend to and look for God's active and loving presence in the midst of all experiences. Second, centering prayer fosters a receptivity to God's will in the world. Practitioners look for God's movement and work in the word. His action is expected, and practitioners surrender to it. Moreover, they actively seek it and look to enter into his rhythms of grace. Keating describes it this way: "Waiting on God in the practice of Centering Prayer strengthens our capacity for interior silence and makes us sensitive to the delicate movements of the spirit in daily life that lead to purification and holiness" (2014, p. 16). The inner space for attentiveness and listening allows us to see God's work in our lives amidst the turmoil of stress and strain.

Centering prayer has four stages which aid in developing the habits of attentiveness and listening. The goal of this spiritual practice is to develop the *intention* to see God presently and actively in all our experiences—to hear and attend to his direction in our lives. The psychological space opened with centering prayer allows us to accept ourselves and make meaning-driven decisions to follow God where he may lead us. This space is one of the main outcomes of centering prayer, and it allows us to experience God's calling on our lives. God calls us to be present with him. He is our identity. We are his children. Centering prayer opens space in our hearts to surrender to his presence.

We are describing the stages Keating (2014) develops in *Intimacy with God*. The first stage focuses on finding a sacred word to represent our intention to surrender to God's active and loving presence. Notice here, the purpose of the word is to represent our wills, our intentions, and it does not represent God. You could choose a word like, "Abba," or "father" to represent your willingness to surrender to God's active and loving presence in your experience.

The second stage emphasizes the experience of rest, of spending time with the word. Over time, emotional space is opened as we spend time with the sacred word. In this step, focus on breathing and sitting silently while reciting the sacred word. As your thoughts wander, gently reintroduce the sacred word. As more time is spent with the word, rest is experienced. We can feel relaxed. We can experience peace and silence. It is here where we experience rest as our worries and concerns fade to the background. This experience is often accompanied by silence. It may also correspond to sensing God's presence.

Stage three focuses on what happens after experiencing God's rest. Once we develop an attitude of inner peace, stillness, receptivity, and silence, sometimes negative thoughts or experiences emerge. That is, the psychological space opened with spending time in rest with the sacred word allows for distractions to lesson. When this space develops, God often brings to our awareness aspects of our past that haven't been dealt with; this process of "unloading," as Keating calls it, means that all the experiences, stresses, and frustrations we have been ignoring or minimizing have space to emerge. Unloading in this manner is a sign we are developing inner peace and silence consenting to see God in our experiences, even when those experiences are trying.

The fourth stage focuses on processing these experiences in God's presence. Evacuation, as Keating describes this step, focuses on processing and eliminating the repressed materials that emerged in step three. We take these memories and experiences to God, who is active and present in the process. We surrender to his loving and active presence in both the positive and negative experiences that emerge in step three. In surrendering and seeing God as present in experience, space is evacuated so we can more deeply and clearly see his presence in our lives.

In general, centering prayer fosters a deep, heart level surrender to God. This surrender is based on consenting to his loving and active presence. Through the sacred word, we surrender to God. We begin to calm the heart, slow down the mind, and focus on God's presence. As distractions arise, we return to the sacred word to refocus our intention to God. Over time and practice, we experience more and more rest which allows for God to bring our pain and struggles to mind. In unloading these experiences, God allows us to see him at work in our lives.

General Suggestions for Centering Prayer

Keating (2014) describes four general strategies for centering prayer. First, select a sacred word. This should be a sacred word for you, and it should represent your intention to see God's active and loving presence at work in your experience. This sacred word is used to gently recenter one's intention should any distractions arise during the prayer.

Second, focus on breathing at the beginning of the practice. Intentional breathing, like what we suggest with *lectio divina*, allows you to settle in. It allows you to begin slowing things down. You should sit comfortably and close your eyes. Begin repeating the sacred word to yourself.

Third, be gentle when distractions arise. When we are meditating, our thoughts can distract us from being still and silent. When we notice our thoughts, gently refocus on the sacred word. The sacred word is intended to recenter our intention on God's active and loving presence. Needing the sacred word or being distracted is not a judgment against you. It is normal. Simply return to the sacred word.

As you complete the prayer, remain in silence for a few moments with your eyes closed. Remember that you may be experiencing unloading and evacuation (as described above) and need a few moments to collect yourself. This is also normal. Centering prayer is a discipline, and it allows you to see God at work in you—both the good and bad, all that you are. This process should take twenty to thirty minutes. Allow yourself space and grace as you begin to notice God's active and loving presence in your experience.

Centering Prayer Follow-Up

Like the other practices described in this chapter, we recommend journaling to process your experiences with centering prayer. In the beginning, you may feel frustrated or bored with this practice! That is normal. It takes time and effort to settle your thoughts. We are constantly distracted; our society seems to thrive on it. Intentionally working on reducing distractions will be challenging. Additionally, our internal distractions are there for a reason. We distract ourselves from the pain and trauma we are experiencing. We hide from the pain of our past. Centering prayer is a process where we allow God to bring these experiences to our awareness so they can be processed. Processing these experiences allows us to experience him more fully as our Savior.

When journaling, focus on two broad questions. First, generally describe your experiences with centering prayer. Reflect on how the process is going. Think about how you experience the process—frustrating, fun, peaceful. Again, there is no judgment here; just describe your experience.

The second broad area for your centering prayer journal focuses on your relationship with God. Reflect on how centering prayer has impacted your relationship with God. Think about how you have changed regarding your intention to surrender to God. Notice any changes in your receptivity and listening towards God and his direction for you. Reflect on how centering prayer impacts your experience of pastoral burnout.

Christian Spiritual Practices for Managing Burnout

This chapter has reviewed three important spiritual practices designed to aid you in coping with pastoral burnout. The Jesus Prayer allows you to focus on your breathing during times of acute stress. Tying your breath with the Jesus Prayer reminds you to pray without ceasing as Paul admonishes us (1 Thess 5:17). *Lectio divina* allows you to center on the word of God. You use *lectio divina* to transform your soul using God's word and your imagination. Centering prayer sharpens the intention to surrender to God's active and loving presence. These three practices can aid you by reinvigorating your spirit.

9

Developing a Plan to Manage Your Burnout

Introduction

THE GOAL OF THIS chapter is to develop a personal plan to cope with pastoral burnout. The main areas associated with pastoral burnout focus on the experience of burnout, the family context of it, the congregation contributions to it, and the organizational structure of the church. The first step in developing this plan is to assess your current levels of burnout. Next, we need to think about the sources of this burnout—conflict between the family and the congregation (time demands and expectations), and the congregation (organizational) contributions. By reflecting on the levels and sources of burnout, we can tailor a spiritually focused plan to address the different sources of pastoral burnout.

Pastors will be encouraged to complete a self-care plan using the information and prompts provided in this chapter. There will be places where pastors can refer back to previous chapters identifying specific Christian and mindfulness practices to cope with specific aspects of pastoral burnout.

Developing a Plan to Manage Your Burnout

This chapter provides important tools for developing a personal approach to address burnout as a pastor. To begin this process, it is important to identify whether and how much you are experiencing burnout now. A great beginning of developing insight into understanding your current level of burnout is reflected in a series of questions. Let's begin by reflecting on your levels and sources of pastoral burnout.

Pastor Self-Assessment of Burnout

The following ten questions are meant as a self-assessment for pastors. This self-assessment is not intended for diagnostic purposes. Instead, these items are useful for pastors to reflect on their experience of burnout in ministry.

Directions: Please indicate the frequency you have experienced each of these *over the past six (6) months*, using the scale of 1 to 5. A score of 1 means never, 2 means seldom, 3 means sometimes, 4 means frequently, and 5 means all the time. Please select N/A if the item does not apply to your experience in ministry. Circle the number next to each question and then add the scores together when you have answered all the questions. Scores from 55 to 65 may *indicate pastoral burnout*. Scores from 45 to 55 may *indicate a higher level of stress* as a pastor. Scores less than 30 indicate some stress, but not a pastor who is burning out.

Table 2. Self-Assessment Burnout Questions.

Question	1 = Never	2 = Seldom	3 = Sometimes	4 = Frequently	5 = All the Time	N/A = Not Applicable

I am increasingly frustrated by my congregation.	I am noticing a more judgmental attitude toward my congregation.	I feel spiritually depleted after engaging in church ministry.	I am drained after meeting with a church member.	I notice that I am responding curtly to my congregation.	I feel emotionally drained after ministering to a church member.
1 = Never	1 = Never	1 = Never	1 = Never	1 = Never	1 = Never
2 = Seldom	2 = Seldom	2 = Seldom	2 = Seldom	2 = Seldom	2 = Seldom
3 = Sometimes	3 = Sometimes	3 = Sometimes	3 = Sometimes	3 = Sometimes	3 = Sometimes
4 = Frequently	4 = Frequently	4 = Frequently	4 = Frequently	4 = Frequently	4 = Frequently
5 = All the Time	5 = All the Time	5 = All the Time	5 = All the Time	5 = All the Time	5 = All the Time
N/A = Not Applicable	N/A = Not Applicable	N/A = Not Applicable	N/A = Not Applicable	N/A = Not Applicable	N/A = Not Applicable

Developing a Plan to Manage Your Burnout

I don't feel the ministry support I need from my supervisor.	Is it draining to work with the person(s) with oversight/authority over you?	I am exhausted after ministering to others.	Responding to my congregation is draining to me.	Ministry is growing less and less important to me.	I am growing more and more indifferent towards the needs of my congregation.
1 = Never	1 = Never	1 = Never	1 = Never	1 = Never	1 = Never
2 = Seldom	2 = Seldom	2 = Seldom	2 = Seldom	2 = Seldom	2 = Seldom
3 = Sometimes	3 = Sometimes	3 = Sometimes	3 = Sometimes	3 = Sometimes	3 = Sometimes
4 = Frequently	4 = Frequently	4 = Frequently	4 = Frequently	4 = Frequently	4 = Frequently
5 = All the Time	5 = All the Time	5 = All the Time	5 = All the Time	5 = All the Time	5 = All the Time
N/A = Not Applicable	N/A = Not Applicable	N/A = Not Applicable	N/A = Not Applicable	N/A = Not Applicable	N/A = Not Applicable

I feel like I am simply going through the motions in ministry.	1 = Never	2 = Seldom	3 = Sometimes	4 = Frequently	5 = All the Time	N/A = Not Applicable

What do you think about your score from the assessment above? Did your score align with your expectations?

Space for Personal Assessment Reflection Questions

In the space provided, please include your responses to the self-assessment above, and respond to the prompts.

1.) In reviewing your scores, where are you on the range? Did your score surprise you? Shock you?

2.) Which of the thirteen questions above reflects your experience the most? Why?

3.) Please describe how you experience your score. What does it feel like for you being a pastor with the score you had?

4.) Write a ministry experience that you have had in the past six months that demonstrates your level of pastoral burnout. Based on what you have read, what are some Christian spiritual practices that could help you cope with this experience?

Developing a Plan to Manage Your Burnout

5.) How does your level of burnout reflect your calling as a pastor? How personally meaningful is your ministry in your congregation?

The Family and Congregation Context of Pastoral Burnout

One of the central arguments of our book is that pastoral burnout is unique when compared to the burnout experiences in other careers. The unique context for the pastor and his family living among the congregation presents challenges that other careers do not face. The pastor's family is often viewed as an ancillary ministry partner for the church. Need a women's ministry director, there's pastor's wife. Need help with the worship team, send the pastor's kid that plays guitar.

Work-family conflict is attributed to the incompatibility of time, lack of resources, competing demands, excessive workload, and other responsibilities between work and family (Sadiq, 2022; Mousavinia et al., 2020). This conflict can lead to high levels of stress, anxiety, depressive symptoms, and burnout, as work-family conflict is a predictor of job satisfaction and job stress (Siswanto et al., 2022; Yu & Li, 2020). In chapter 5 we discussed the impact congregational expectations and boundary violations have on the pastor and family. In thinking about expectations, often the pastor's family has higher and more rigid behavioral and participation expectations when compared with other families in the congregation. These often-unspoken expectations lead to conflict between the pastor's family and congregation. This conflict impacts everyone at the church.

On top of the unspoken expectations, boundary violations occur. These are times where the pastor is with his family and a member of the congregation interrupts that time. These boundary violations are often due to legitimate and pressing concerns—emergencies that need the pastor's spiritual support. Sometimes these violations are less important, yet the member still interrupts the pastor's family time.

Space for Personal Reflection on Family and Congregation Questions

1.) As the pastor, how have you experienced conflict between your family and congregation?

2.) How have unspoken expectations for your family caused conflict at home? What did you do to manage these expectations?

3.) As the pastor, how have you experienced congregational interruptions of your time with your family? What do you do when you experience these types of boundary violations?

4.) In reflecting on chapters 7 and 8, what are some of the Christian spiritual and mindfulness practices you could use to cope with this stress?

The following questions stem from Maslach's (1997, p. 160) six areas of organizational life, which are defined below:

Developing a Plan to Manage Your Burnout

- Workload: The extent to which demands are manageable or overwhelming
- Control: Amount of control people feel in their jobs
- Reward: The effectiveness of rewards and recognition systems
- Community: The organization's responsiveness to staff and community
- Fairness: Respect and fairness among people in the organization
- Values: Personal and organizational values about work

The following set of questions is intended for you to understand the possible causes of your stress and burnout, as well as to help you think about the organizational structure of your church. In other words, the focus of this set of questions is the church as a contributor or cause of a pastor experiencing burnout. Based upon the previous assessments in this chapter, is the church at which you are called to serve causing you to experience burnout? Pastors may experience burnout from the structure of the church, leadership, and the congregation. Which of these three causes you the most stress? The following questions are intended to help you reflect on the organizational life of the church where you pastor.

- Are your ministry work demands manageable or overwhelming based upon the time you're allotted to complete them in a given day?
    - o Are you continually pulled from your pastoral duties to complete tasks that are urgent?
    - o Does your church support the delegation of ministerial responsibilities?
    - o Do you have work-life balance?
- Do you have autonomy to complete your work tasks as you want to complete them?
    - o How do you decide which ministry demands are most important at a given time?

- Do you feel that you are micromanaged?
- Are you adequately rewarded and recognized for the work you perform?
  - What type of rewards and recognition do you receive for your work?
- Is your church responsive to your work-related requests?
  - Do you have elders, deacons, and other church leaders to share the ministry burden?
  - Would your church grant you a sabbatical?
- Do you feel as though you are an integral part of your church community?
  - Does your church have unreasonable expectations of your spouse and children?
- Would you characterize your church's work environment as being fair and respectful?
- Do your personal values align with your church's values?
  - What are your personal values?
  - What are your church's values?

By honestly answering these questions and incorporating the coping mechanisms in this chapter you can formalize a plan that is specific to your responsibilities and level of stress. What steps can you take to get help in coping with pastoral burnout? What are three takeaways from this chapter that you can implement in the week? Take the time to write these takeaways down and put the piece of paper somewhere you can see it every day. Visualize the positive changes that would result from these three takeaways. As always, pray for God to be with you.

Developing a Plan to Manage Your Burnout

Space for Self-Reflection on the Congregation and Pastoral Burnout:

1. In reflecting on your workload, how stressed are you about completing your tasks?

2. How do your other ministry obligations impact your sermon prep? Do you feel like you are constantly being interrupted when preparing your sermon?

3. How do your elders/deacons/church board respond when you discuss your stress levels and workload?

4. In reviewing our chapters on Christian spirituality and mindfulness, are there any practices that you could use to deal with stress from the congregation? Are there any rest-taking practices that could aid you?

Developing the Pastor's Personal Burnout Plan

Now it is your turn to think about developing a short-term and long-term plan to deal with pastoral burnout. We recommend beginning a practice of daily journaling that allows you to track your progress on your personal pastoral burnout plan. It is important to regularly practice the disciplines and practices we discussed in earlier chapters. Your practice allows these disciplines to invigorate and reconnect you with God. Practicing them daily will develop the spiritual muscles needed to cope with any stressor that arises during the course of ministry.

Step One for Developing Your Personal Plan

To begin this process, review the responses to the three broad areas of reflection questions earlier in the chapter. Flip back and read over your answers to the self-assessment. As you gain insight into your experience of pastoral burnout, it will provide the source for the plan you are building. This is important as burnout in general, and especially pastoral burnout, are a spiritual depletion problem (*acedia* as described in chapter 2). We will need spiritual resources to cope with this spiritual condition.

Step one is to respond to the reflection questions from earlier in the chapter. We recommend doing this response in your daily journal. We recommend beginning your journal with this reflection so that it will guide you every day in identifying (1) a potential source of pastoral burnout, (2) remind you of a specific short-term or long-term spiritual strategy to cope with the situation causing burnout, and (3) allow you to track your progress in coping with pastoral burnout.

Step Two for Developing Your Personal Plan

Identify at least one short-term and one long-term spiritual strategy that you identified in your personal reflections above. If you had trouble specifically identifying a spiritual practice in the self-reflection, review the materials in chapters 6, 7, and 8 that describe several different Christian and mindfulness practices to cope with stress. This part of your journal should identify one or two short-term practices—saying the Jesus Prayer—and one or two more long-term practices—*lectio divina*—each day. You should record the specific practice and what you learned about yourself and your experience of pastoral burnout from the experience. Ideally, these practices should be tailored to address the nuances of your self-reflections. Additionally, some practices may fit your personality and church tradition better than others, and we recommend you begin with those practices.

Step Three for Developing Your Personal Plan

Do your plan. Regularly and intentionally devote yourself to the daily work you developed in steps one and two. We recommend using this plan as your personal devotion time every day. Practicing short-term and long-term spiritual disciplines will aid you in developing resources for coping with pastoral burnout when you experience stressors in your ministry.

Step Four of Developing Your Personal Plan

Regularly reflect on your progress. Revisit this chapter occasionally, at least once a month, to conduct regular self-assessments. Your experience of pastoral burnout may shift over time and in the ebbs and flows of the life of your local congregation. The focus of these self-assessments is to gauge how the spiritual disciplines you identified are addressing the specific contours of your experience of pastoral burnout. Additionally, this self-reflection should focus on how the spiritual disciplines are working in your daily life to reconnect you with God. Remember that pastoral burnout is a spiritual depletion problem and requires spiritual rejuvenation.

A Sample Template for Your Personal Burnout Plan

This template is available at our website, Center for Pastoral Renewal: https://centerforpastoralrenewal.com/resources/.

Date:

Step One: Self Reflection Responses

- Step one: Self-assessment reflection: We recommend using the self-assessment tool from our website here: https://centerforpastoralrenewal.com/resources/
- Step one: Family and congregation reflection
    - As the pastor, how have you experienced conflict between your family and congregation?

    - _____
    - _____
    - _____
    - _____

    - How have unspoken expectations for your family caused conflict at home? What did you do to manage these expectations?

    - _____
    - _____
    - _____
    - _____

    - As the pastor, how have you experienced congregational interruptions of your time with your family? What do you do when you experience these types of boundary violations?

    - _____
    - _____
    - _____
    - _____

Developing a Plan to Manage Your Burnout

- What are some of the Christian spiritual and mindfulness practices you could use to cope with this stress?

  - _____
  - _____
  - _____
  - _____

- Step one: Congregation reflection
  - Are your ministry work demands manageable or overwhelming based upon the time you're allotted to complete them in a given day?
  - Are you continually pulled from your pastoral duties to complete tasks that are urgent?

    - _____
    - _____
    - _____
    - _____

  - Does your church support the delegation of ministerial responsibilities?

    - _____
    - _____
    - _____
    - _____

  - Do you have work-life balance?

    - _____
    - _____
    - _____
    - _____

- Do you have autonomy to complete your work tasks as you want to complete them?
- How do you decide which ministry demands are most important at a given time?
- Do you feel that you are micromanaged?

- _____
- _____
- _____
- _____

- Are you adequately rewarded and recognized for the work you perform?
- What type of rewards and recognition do you receive for your work?

- _____
- _____
- _____
- _____

- Is your church responsive to your work-related requests?
- Do you have elders, deacons, and other church leaders to share the ministry burden?
- Would your church grant you a sabbatical?

- _____
- _____
- _____
- _____

Step Two: Christian Spiritual and Mindfulness Practices

o Step Two: Short-term practices

- _____
- _____
- _____
- _____

o Step Two: Long-term practices

- _____
- _____
- _____
- _____

Step Three: Reflect on Daily Practice

o Step three: How consistently am I doing my daily short-term and long-term practices?

- _____
- _____
- _____
- _____

o Step three: How well do the practices I picked develop or increase my connection with God?

- _____
- _____
- _____
- _____

Step four: Reflect on Progress

- Step four: Am I meeting my practice goals?
  - _____
  - _____
  - _____
  - _____

- Step four: Did the practices I picked help me reconnect with God?
  - _____
  - _____
  - _____
  - _____

- Step four: Are the practices I picked addressing the areas I identified in my self-reflection in step one?
  - _____
  - _____
  - _____
  - _____

- Step four: Are there any revisions to my plan needed based on my progress? (At least once a month)
  - _____
  - _____
  - _____
  - _____

Conclusions

This chapter provides you with suggestions and steps to develop a plan for coping with pastoral burnout. This plan allows you to gain insight into your experience of pastoral burnout. It also aids you in connecting specific Christian spiritual and mindfulness practices with your unique experiences of burnout. We pray that this plan and our book will aid you in coping with pastoral burnout.

References

Adams, J. E. (1986). *The biblical view of self-esteem, self-love, and self-image* [Kindle edition]. Harvest House.

Allen, T. D., and Martin, A. (2017). The work-family interface: A retrospective look at 20 years of research in JOHP. *Journal of Occupational and Health Psychology*, 22, 259–72. DOI: 10.1037/ocp0000065.

Al-Refae, M., Al-Refae, A., Munroe, M., Sardella, N. A., & Ferrari, M. (2021). A self-compassion and mindfulness-based cognitive mobile intervention (serene) for depression, anxiety, and stress: Promoting adaptive emotional regulation and wisdom. *Frontiers in Psychology*, 12, 648087–648087. doi.org/10.3389/fpsyg.2021.648087.

Anderson, R. S. (1997). *The soul of ministry*. John Knox.

Aponte, H. J. (2003). Spirituality: The heart of therapy. In T. D. Carlson & M. J. Erickson (Eds.), *Spirituality and family therapy* (pp. 13–27). Haworth.

Ashforth, B. E. (1989). The experience of powerlessness in organizations. *Organizational Behavior and Human Decision Processes*, 43(2), 207–42.

Ashforth, B. E., & Humphrey, R. H. (1993). Emotional labor in service roles: The influence of identity. *Academy of Management*, 18(1), 88–115. https://doi.org/10.5465/amr.1993.3997508

Barna Group. (2017, April 6). Meet the "Spiritual but Not Religious." Retrieved May 2, 2023, from https://www.barna.com/research/meet-spiritual-not-religious/.

Blanck, P., Perleth, S., Heidenreich, T., Kröger, P., Ditzen, B., Bents, H., & Johannes Mander, J. (2018). Effects of mindfulness exercises as stand-alone intervention on symptoms of anxiety and depression: Systematic review and meta-analysis. *Behaviour Research and Therapy*, 102, 25–35. doi.org/10.1016/j.brat.2017.12.002.

Blanton, P. G. (2011). The other mindful practice: Centering prayer and psychotherapy. *Pastoral Psychology*, 60, 133–47. DOI: 10.1007/s11089-010-0292-9.

Blanton, P. G. (2021). *Centering prayer: A contemplative path to virtuous living*. Orbis.

References

Boersma, H. (2023). *Pierced by love: Divine reading with the Christian tradition.* Lexham.

Brotheridge, C. M. (1999). Unwrapping the black box: A test of why emotional labour may lead to emotional exhaustion. In D. Miller (Ed.), *Proceedings of the Administrative Sciences Association of Canada (Organizational Behaviour Division)* (pp. 11–20). New Brunswick.

Brotheridge, C., & Grandey, A. (2002). Emotional labour and burnout: Comparing two perspectives of "people work." *Journal of Vocational Behavior, 60*(1), 7–39.

Brotheridge, C. M., & Lee, R. T. (1998). On the dimensionality of emotional labour: Development and validation of the Emotional Labour Scale. Paper presented at the First Conference on Emotions in Organizational Life, San Diego.

Burch, T. (2020). All in the family: The link between couple-level work-family conflict and family satisfaction and its impact on the composition of the family over time. *Journal of Business and Psychology, 35*(5), 593–607. https://doi.org/10.1007/s10869-019-09641-y.

Burke, P. J. (1991). Identity processes and social stress. *American Sociological Review, 56*(6), 836–49. DOI: 10.2307/2096259.

Carlson, L. E., Speca, M., Faris, P., & Patel, K. D. (2007). One year pre–post intervention follow-up of psychological, immune, endocrine and blood pressure outcomes of mindfulness-based stress reduction (MBSR) in breast and prostate cancer outpatients. *Brain, Behavior and Immunity, 21*(8), 1038–49. https://doi.org/10.1016/j.bbi.2007.04.002.

Carlson, T. D., & Erickson, M. J. (2003). A conversation about spirituality in marriage and family therapy: Exploring the possibilities. In T. D. Carlson & M. J. Erickson (Eds.), *Spirituality and family therapy* (pp. 1–11). Haworth.

Cavanagh, K., Strauss, C., Cicconi, F., Griffiths, N., Wyper, A., & Jones, F. (2013). A randomised controlled trial of a brief online mindfulness-based intervention. *Behaviour Research and Therapy, 51*(9), 573–78. https://doi.org/10.1016/j.brat.2013.06.003.

Cherniss, C. (1993). The role of professional self-efficacy in the etiology and amelioration of burnout. In W. B. Schaufeli, C. Maslach, & T. Marek (Eds.), *Professional burnout: Recent developments in theory and research* (pp. 135–49). Taylor & Francis.

Choi Y. G., and Kim, K. Y. (2015). A literature review of emotional labor and emotional labor strategies. *Universal Journal of Management 3*(7): 283–90.

Cloud, H., & Townsend, J. (2017). *Boundaries: When to say yes, how to say no to take control of your life* (2nd ed.). Zondervan.

Coe, J. H. (2019). The controversy over contemplation and contemplative prayer: An historical, theological, and biblical resolution. In J. H. Coe and K. Strobel (Eds.), *Embracing contemplation: Reclaiming a Christian spiritual practice.* IVP Academic.

Cordes, C. L., & Dougherty, T. W. (1993). A review and an integration of research on job burnout. *Academy of Management Review, 18*(4), 621–56.

References

Dane, E. (2011). Paying attention to mindfulness and its effects on task performance in the workplace. *Journal of Management, 37,* 997–1018.

DeLamater, J. D., Myers, D. J., and Collett, J. (2014). *Social Psychology* (8th ed). Westview.

Demarest, B. (2012). Introduction. In B. Demarest (Ed.). *Four views on Christian spirituality* (pp. 11–25). Zondervan.

Dunbar, S., Frederick, T., Thai, Y., & Gill, J. (2020). Calling, caring, and connecting burnout in Christian ministry. *Mental Health, Religion & Culture,* 173–86. https://doi.org/10.1080/13674676.2020.1744548.

Erickson, R. J. & Wharton, A. S. (1997). Inauthenticity and depression: Assessing the consequences of interactive service work. *Work and Occupation, 24*(2), 188–213.

Flook, L., Goldberg, S. B., Pinger, L., Bonus, K., & Davidson, R. J. (2013). Mindfulness for teachers: A pilot study to assess effects on stress, burnout, and teaching efficacy. *Mind, Brain and Education, 7*(3), 182–95. DOI: 10.1111/mbe.12026.

Foster, R. J. (1998). *Streams of living water: Celebrating the great traditions of Christian faith.* Harper.

Foster, R. J. (2011). *Sanctuary of the soul: Journey into meditative prayer* (Kindle ed.). Renovare Resources.

Fowler, J. (1995). *Stages of faith: The psychology of human development.* San Francisco.

Francis, L. J., Laycock, P., & Ratter, H. (2019). Testing the Francis burnout inventory among Anglican clergy in England. *Mental Health, Religion & Culture, 22*(10), 1057–67. https://doi.org/10.1080/13674676.2019.1644304.

Francis, L. J., Village, A., Robbins, M., & Wulff, K. (2011). Work-related psychological health among clergy serving in the presbyterian church (USA): Testing the idea of balanced affect. *Review of Religious Research, 53*(1), 9–22. https://doi.org/10.1007/s13644-011-0003-8.

Francis, L., Laycock, P., & Brewster, C. (2017). Work-related psychological wellbeing: Testing the balanced affect model among Anglican clergy. *Religions, 8*(7), 118. https://doi.org/10.3390/rel8070118.

Frederick, T. V., & Dunbar, S. E. (2019). *A Christian approach to work and family burnout: Calling, caring, and connecting.* Lexington.

Frederick, T. V., & Dunbar, S. E. (2022). *Identity, calling, and workplace spirituality: Meaning making and developing career fit.* Lexington.

Frederick, T. V., Dunbar, S., Purrington, S., Fischer, S., & Ardito, R. (2018). Exploring the relative contributions of differentiation of self and mindfulness for predicting burnout. In L. Brewer (Ed.), *Meditation: Practice, Techniques, and Health Benefits* (pp. 185–204). Nova Science.

Frederick, T. V., Dunbar, S., & Thai, Y. (2018). Burnout in Christian perspective. *Pastoral Psychology, 67,* pp. 267–76. DOI: 10.1007/s11089-017-0799-4

References

Frederick, T., Thai, Y., & Dunbar, S. (2021). Coping with pastoral burnout using Christian contemplative practices. *Religions, 12*(378), 1–13. https://doi.org/10.3390/rel12060378.

Frederick, T. V., Thai, Y., Dunbar, S. E., Ardito, R., Eichler, K., Kidd, K., Carrera, J., & Almero, M. (2023). The effects of role differentiation among clergy: Impact on pastoral burnout and job satisfaction. *Pastoral Psychology, 72*(1), 121–42. https://doi.org/10.1007/s11089-022-01052-w.

Friedman, E. (1985). *From generation to generation: Family process in church and synagogue.* Guilford.

Garzon, F. (2013). Christian devotional meditation for anxiety. In E. Worthington, E. Johnson, J. Hook, & J. Aten (Eds.), *Evidence-based practices for Christian counseling and psychotherapy* (pp. 59–80). InterVarsity.

Gilbert, R. M. (2006). *The eight concepts of Bowen theory.* Leading Systems.

Glomb, T. M., Duffy, M. K., Bono, J. E., & Yang, T. (2011). Mindfulness at work. In A. Joshi, J. Martocchio, & H. Liao (Eds.), *Research in personnel and human resources management* (pp. 115–57). (Research in Personnel and Human Resources Management, vol. 30). https://doi.org/10.1108/S0742-7301(2011)0000030005.

Grabovac, A. D., Lau, M. A., Willett, B. R. (2011). Mechanisms of mindfulness: A Buddhist psychological model. *Mindfulness, 2,* 154–66.

Grandey, A. A. (2000). Emotion regulation in the workplace: A new way to conceptualize emotional labor. *Journal of Occupational Health Psychology, 5,* 95–110.

Greenhaus, J. H., & Beutell, N. J. (1985). Sources of conflict between work and family roles. *Academy of Management Review, 10,* 76–88.

Greenhaus, J. H., Collins, K., & Shaw, J. (2003). The relation between work-family balance and quality of life. *Journal of Vocational Behavior, 63,* 510–31. DOI: 10.1016/S0001-8791(02)00042-8.

Greenhaus, J. H., & Powell, G. H. (2006). When work and family are allies: A theory of work family enrichment. *Academy of Management Review, 31,* 72–92.

Grzywacz, J. G., & Carlson, D. S. (2007). Conceptualizing work—family balance: Implications for practice and research. *Advances in Developing Human Resources, 9*(4), 455–71. doi.org/10.1177/1523422307305487.

Hall, C. M. (1991). *The Bowen family theory and its uses.* Jason Aronson.

Hawley, L. L., Schwartz, D., Bieling, P. J., Irving, J., Corcoran, K., Farb, N. A. S., Anderson, A., & Segal, Z. V. (2014). Mindfulness practice, rumination and clinical outcome in mindfulness-based treatment. *Cognitive Therapy and Research, 38*(1), 1–9. DOI: 10.1007/s10608-013-9586-4.

Hester, J. A. (2017). *Stress and longevity in pastoral ministry: A phenomenological study* [Unpublished doctoral dissertation]. Southern Baptist Theological Seminary.

Hill, C. L. M., & Updegraff, J. A. (2012). Mindfulness and its relationship to emotional regulation. *Emotion, 12*(1), 81–90. DOI: 10.1037/a0026355

Hochschild, A. R. (1983). *The managed heart.* University of California Press.

References

Hochschild, A. R. (2012). *The managed heart* (3rd ed.). University of California Press.

Horton, M. (2013). *Pilgrim theology: Core doctrines for Christian disciples*. Zondervan.

Hülsheger, U. R., Alberts, H. J., Feinholdt, A., & Lang, J. W. (2013). Benefits of mindfulness at work: The role of mindfulness in emotion regulation, emotional exhaustion, and job satisfaction. *The Journal of Applied Psychology, 98*(2), 310–25. https://doi.org/10.1037/a0031313.

Hunt, C. A., Letzen, J. E., Krimmel, S. R., Burrowes, S. A., Haythornthwaite, J. A., Keaser, M., . . . Seminowicz, D. A. (2023). Meditation practice, mindfulness, and pain-related outcomes in mindfulness-based treatment for episodic migraine. *Mindfulness, 14*(4), 769–83. DOI: 10.1007/s12671-023-02105-8.

Huppertz, A. V., Hülsheger, U. R., De Calheiros Velozo, J., & Schreurs, B. H. (2020). Why do emotional labor strategies differentially predict exhaustion? Comparing psychological effort, authenticity, and relational mechanisms. *Journal of Occupational Health Psychology, 25*(3), 214–26.

Jackson, S. E., Schwab, R. L., & Schuler, R. S. (1986). Toward an understanding of the burnout phenomenon. *Journal of Applied Psychology, 71*(4), 630–40.

Kabat-Zinn, J. (2003). Mindfulness-based interventions in context: Past, present, and future. *Clinical Psychology: Science and Practice, 10*(2), 144–56.

Kabat-Zinn, J. (2013). *Full catastrophe living: Using the wisdom of your body and mind to face stress, pain, and illness* (revised ed.). Bantam.

Kabat-Zinn, J. (2015). Mindfulness. *Orthogonal Rotation in Consciousness, 6*, 1481–83. DOI: 10.1007/s12671-015-0456-x.

Kalliath, T., & Brough, P. (2008). Work-life balance: A review of the meaning of the balance construct. *Journal of Management & Organization, 14*, 323–27.

Keating, T. (2014). *Intimacy with God: An introduction to centering prayer*. Crossroad.

Keller, T., & Keller, K. (2016). *The meaning of marriage: Facing the complexities of commitment with the wisdom of God*. Penguin.

Kim, S.-H., Corbett, T. M., Strenger, N., & Lee, C. (2016). An Actor–Partner Interdependence analysis of the ABC-X stress model among clergy couples. *Psychology of Religion and Spirituality, 8*(1), 65–76. https://doi.org/10.1037/rel0000031.

Knabb, J. J., & Vazquez, V. E. (2018). A randomized controlled trial of a 2-week internet-based contemplative prayer program for Christians with daily stress. *Spirituality in Clinical Practice, 5*(1), 37–53. https://doi.org/10.1037/scp0000154.

Kristensen, T. S., Borritz, M., Villadsen, E., & Christensen, K. B. (2005). The Copenhagen Burnout Inventory: A new tool for the assessment of burnout. *Work and Stress, 19*(3), 192–207. https://doi.org/10.1080/02678370500297720

References

Lange, S., & Rowold, J. (2019). Mindful leadership: Evaluation of a mindfulness-based leader intervention. *Gruppe. Interaktion. Organisation, 50*, 319-35.

Larson E. B., & Yao, X. (2005). Clinical empathy as emotional labor in the patient-physician relationship. *JAMA, 293*(9), 1100-6. DOI: 10.1001/jama.293.9.1100.

Lashley, C. (2005). Emotional labor. In *International encyclopedia of hospitality management* (pp. 186–88). Routledge.

Lee, C. (1995). Rethinking boundary ambiguity from an ecological perspective: Stress in Protestant clergy families. *Family Process, 34*(1). https://doi.org/10.1111/j.1545-5300.1995.00075.x.

Lee, C. (1999). Specifying intrusive demands and their outcomes in congregational ministry: A report on the Ministry Demands Inventory. *Journal for the Scientific Study of Religion, 38*(4). https://doi.org/10.2307/1387607.

Lee, C. (2007). Patterns of stress and support among Adventist clergy: Do pastors and their spouses differ? *Pastoral Psychology, 55*(6), 761–71. https://doi.org/10.1007/s11089-007-0086-x.

Lee, C., & Balswick, J. O. (1989). *Life in a glass house: The minister's family in its unique social context*. Zondervan. Reprinted in 2006 by Fuller Seminary Press.

Lee, C., & Balswick, J. O. (2006). *Life in a glass house: The minister's family and the local congregation*. Fuller Seminary Press.

Lee, C., and Iverson-Gilbert, J. (2003). Demand, support, and perception in family-related stress among Protestant clergy. *Family Relations, 52*(3), 249–57. https://doi.org/10.1111/j.1741-3729.2003.00249.x.

Lee Lloyd Johnson, R. (2019). A brief history of mindfulness in addictions treatment. *International Journal for the Advancement of Counselling, 41*(2), 284–95. DOI: 10.1007/s10447-019-09372-y.

Lee, M., & Jang, K.-S. (2021). Nursing students' meditative and sociocognitive mindfulness, achievement emotions, and academic outcomes. *Nurse Educator, 46*(3), E39–E44. DOI: 10.1097/NNE.0000000000000902.

Leiter, M. P., & Maslach, C. (1988). The impact of interpersonal environment on burnout and organizational commitment. *Journal of Organizational Behavior, 9*(4), 297-308.

Lennard, A. C., Scott, B. A., & Johnson, R. E. (2019). Turning frowns (and smiles) upside down: A multilevel examination of surface acting positive and negative emotions on well-being. *Journal of Applied Psychology, 104*, 1164–80.

Marcussen, K. (2006). Identities, self-esteem, and psychological distress: An application of identity-discrepancy theory. *Sociological Perspectives, 49*(1), 1–24. DOI: 10.1525/sop.2006.49.1.1.

Maslach, C., Jackson, S., & Leiter, M. (1996). *Maslach Burnout Inventory Manual*. (3rd ed.), 1–45. Mind Garden.

Maslach, C., & Leiter, M. (1997). *The truth about burnout: How organizations cause personal stress and what to do about it*. Jossey-Bass.

References

Maslach, C., Schaufeli, W. B., & Leiter, M. P. (2001). Job burnout. *Annual Review of Psychology*, 52(1), 397–422.

Maxon, R. (1999). *Stress in the workplace: A costly epidemic*. Fairleigh Dickinson University Magazine. Retrieved February 15, 2023, from http://www.fdu.edu/newspubs/magazine/99su/stress.html.

McGrath, A. E. (1999). *Christian spirituality: An introduction*. Blackwell.

McNulty, D. S., LaMonica-Way, C., & Senneff, J.-A. (2022). The impact of mindfulness on stress and burnout of new graduate nurses as a component of a nurse residency program. *Journal of Nursing Administration*, 52(4), E12–E18. DOI: 10.1097/NNA.0000000000001137.

Miller, R. B., Anderson, S., & Keala, D. K. (2004). Is Bowen theory valid? A review of basic research. *Journal of Marital and Family Therapy*, 30(4), 453–66. doi.org/10.1111/j.1752-0606.2004.tb01255.x.

Moceri, J., & Cox, P. H. (2019). Mindfulness-based practice to reduce blood pressure and stress in priests. *Journal for Nurse Practitioners*, 15(6), 115–17. DOI: 10.1016/j.nurpra.2019.01.001.

Mousavinia, S., Naami, A., Arshadi, N., & Beshlideh, K. (2020). The role of employees' wellbeing in reducing the effects of work-family conflict on family satisfaction, parenting quality, and couple relationship quality in nurses. *Iran Journal of Nursing*, 33(124), 41–57. https://web.archive.org/web/20220802040936id_/https://ijn.iums.ac.ir/files/site1/user_files_e64ade/mohammadjavad-A-10-2512-2-22d0b8e.pdf.

Nelson, A. S. (2023). *A change of heart*. Free Grace.

Nguyen, M. C., Gabbe, S. G., Kemper, K. J., Mahan, J. D., Cheavens, J. S., & Moffatt-Bruce, S. D. (2020). Training on mind-body skills: Feasibility and effects on physician mindfulness, compassion, and associated effects on stress, burnout, and clinical outcomes. *Journal of Positive Psychology*, 15(2), 194–207. DOI: 10.1080/17439760.2019.1578892.

Oman, D. (2013). Defining religion and spirituality. In R. F. Paloutzian and C. L. Park (Eds.), *Handbook of the psychology of religion and spirituality* (2nd ed.) (pp. 23–47). Guilford.

Pargament, K. I. (1992). Of means and ends: Religion and the search for significance. *International Journal for the Psychology of Religion*, 2, 201–29.

Physician Practice Perspectives. (2016). Employee retention a bigger challenge in growing economy. *Physician Practice Perspectives*, 8–10.

Pugliesi, K., & Shook, S. L. (1997). Gender, jobs, and emotional labor in a complex organization. In R. J. Erickson and B. Cuthbertson-Johnson (Eds.), *Social Perspectives on Emotion*, vol. 4, pp. 283–316. JAI.

Rafaeli, A., & Sutton, R. I. (1987). Expression of emotion as part of the work role. *Academy of Management Review*, 12(1), 23–37. https://doi.org/10.2307/257991.

Rafaeli, A., & Sutton, R. I. (1989). The expression of emotion in organizational life. *Research in Organizational Behavior*, 11, 1–42.

Rigas, C., Park, H., Nassim, M., Su, C.-L., Greenway, K., Lipman, M., McVeigh, C., Novak, M., Trinh, E., Alam, A., Suri, R. S., Mucsi, I., Torres-Platas,

References

S. G., Noble, H., Sekhon, H., Rej, S., Lifshitz, M. (2022). Long-term effects of a brief mindfulness intervention versus a health enhancement program for treating depression and anxiety in patients undergoing hemodialysis: A randomized controlled trial. *Canadian Journal of Kidney Health and Disease, 9*, 1–11. DOI: 10.1177/20543581221074562.

Rinne, J. (2014). *Church elders: How to shepherd God's people like Jesus*. Crossway.

Romero-Martín, S., Elboj-Saso, C., & Íñiguez-Berrozpe, T. (2022). Burnout and mindfulness among social workers in Spain: A structural equation model of mindfulness and areas of worklife as burnout predictors. *International Social Work.* doi.org/10.1177/00208728221112733.

Sadiq, M. (2022). Policing in pandemic: Is perception of workload causing work–family conflict, job dissatisfaction and job stress? *Journal of Public Affairs, 22*(2), 1–8. https://doi.org/10.1002/pa.2486.

Sauter, S., Murphy, L., Colligan, M., Swanson, N., Hurrell Jr, J., Scharf Jr, F., Grubb, R. S. P., Goldenhar, L., Alterman, T., Johnston, J., Hamilton, A., Tisdale, J. (1999). *STRESS . . . At Work*, 99–101. https://www.cdc.gov/niosh/docs/99-101/.

Sauvain-Sabé, M., Congard, A., Kop, J.-L., Weismann-Arcache, C., & Villieux, A. (2022). The mediating roles of affect and coping strategy in the relationship between trait mindfulness and burnout among French healthcare professionals. *Canadian Journal of Behavioural Science, 55*(1), 34–45. doi.org/10.1037/cbs0000312.

Schaufeli, W. B., Maslach, C., & Marek, T. (1993). The future of burnout. In W. B. Schaufeli, C. Maslach, & T. Marek (Eds.), *Professional burnout: Recent developments in theory and research* (pp. 253–59). Taylor & Francis.

Scott, B. A., & Barnes, C. M. (2011). A multilevel field investigation of emotional labor, affect, work withdrawal, and gender. *Academy of Management Journal, 54*, 116–36.

Shankar, B., & Kumar, S. (2014). *Emotional labor and burnout relationship: Role of social support and coping.* Research Gate.

Siswanto, M., Nur, H., Mutadi, R., & Rifki, H. (2022). Impact of work-family conflict on job satisfaction and job stress: Mediation model from Indonesia. *Problems & Perspectives in Management, 20*(2), 44–56. DOI: 10.21511/ppm.20(2).2022.05.

Smethurst, M. (2021). *Deacons*. Crossway.

Smith, J. A. (2009). *Desiring the kingdom: Worship, worldview, and cultural formation*. Baker Academic.

Talbot, J. M. (2013). *The Jesus Prayer* [Kindle ed.]. InterVarsity.

Titelman, P. (2014). The concept of differentiation of self in Bowen theory. In P. Titelman (Ed.), *Differentiation of self: Bowen family systems perspectives* (pp. 3–64). Routledge.

Trammel, R. C., and Trent, J. T. (2021). *A counselor's guide to Christian mindfulness: Engaging the mind, body, and soul in biblical practices and therapies*. Zondervan.

References

Troy, A. S., Shallcross, A. J., Davis, T. S., Tchiki, D. S., & Mauss, I. B. (2013). History of mindfulness-based cognitive therapy is associated with increased cognitive reappraisal ability. *Mindfulness, 4*(3), 213–22. DOI: 10.1007/s12671-012-0114-5.

Tsang, H. W. H., Chan, E. P., & Cheung, W. M. (2008). Effects of mindful and non-mindful exercises on people with depression: A systematic review. *British Journal of Clinical Psychology, 47*(3), 303–22.

Udipi, S., Veach, P. M., Kao, J., & LeRoy, B. S. (2008). The psychic costs of empathic engagement: Personal and demographic predictors of genetic counselor compassion fatigue. *Journal of Genetic Counseling, 17*(5), 459–71. https://doi.org/10.1007/s10897-008-9162-3.

University of Cambridge. (2011, November 29). *Effects of work-related stress.* https://www.hr.admin.cam.ac.uk/policies-procedures/managing-stress-and-promoting-wellbeing-work-policy/policy-statement/effects.

van der Riet, P., Levett-Jones, T., & Aquino-Russell, C. (2018). The effectiveness of mindfulness meditation for nurses and nursing students: An integrated literature review. *Nurse Education Today, 65,* 201–11. DOI: 10.1016/j.nedt.2018.03.018.

Vazquez, V. E., & Jensen, G. R. (2020). Practicing the Jesus Prayer: Implications for psychological and spiritual well-being. *Journal of Psychology and Christianity, 39*(1), 65–74.

Village, A., Payne, V. J., & Francis, L. J. (2018). Testing the balanced affect model of clergy work-related psychological health: Replication among Anglican clergy in Wales. *Rural Theology, 16*(2), 93–100. DOI: 10.1080/14704994.2018.1519918.

Wharton, A. (2009). The sociology of emotional labor. *The Annual Review of Sociology, 35,* 147–65.

Whitney, D. S. (2014). *Spiritual disciplines for the Christian life* (revised and updated). NavPress.

Wilhoit, J. C. (2014). Contemplative and centering prayer. *Journal of Spiritual Formation and Soul Care, 7*(1), 107–17. https://doi.org/10.1177/193979091400700110.

Wilhoit, J. C., & Howard, E. B. (2012). *Discovering lectio divina: Bringing scripture to ordinary life.* InterVarsity.

Yu, M., & Li, J. (2020). Work-family conflict and mental health among Chinese underground coal miners: The moderating role of psychological capital. *Psychology, Health, & Medicine, 25*(1), 1–9. DOI: 10.1080/13548506.2019.1595686.

Zapf, D. (2002). Emotion work and psychological wellbeing: A review of the literature and some conceptual considerations. *Human Resource Management Review, 12,* 237–68.

Zhang, C., Cheung, S. P., & Huang, C. (2022). Job demands and resources, mindfulness, and burnout among delivery drivers in China. *Frontiers in Psychology, 13,* 1–10. DOI: 10.3389/fpsyg.2022.792254.

Zhang, M., Foley, S., Li, H., and Zhu, J. (2018). Social support, work-family balance and satisfaction among Chinese middle- and upper-level managers: Testing cross-domain and within-domain effects. *International Journal of Human Resource Management, 31*(21), 2714–36. https://doi.org/10.1080/09585192.2018.1464490.

Index

Page references followed by italicized *f* indicates figures; *t*, tables

acedia, 17–18, 38
acting. *See* deep acting; surface acting
Adams, Jay, on self-esteem, 51
anxiety
    as burnout symptom, 24
    emotional processes for management of in families, 55–56
    journaling impacts on, 83
    mindfulness practices impacting, 76
    sleep impacting, 84–85
    work-family conflict and, 109
apathy, 38
apophatic (wordless silence) facet of Christian spirituality, 63–65, 69
approaches to managing burnout
    Christian spiritual traditions, 68–73
    coping with exhaustion, 48–49
    developing a plan, 104–20
    Differentiation in Christ (DifC), 50–58
    Differentiation of Self (DoS), 43–45
    enriching resources, 39
    managing emotional labor, 28–30
    mindfulness approaches, 75–88
    strategies for managing inefficacy, 28–30

balance. *See* work-family balance
Balswick, Jack, 36
behavior, 38
Bible
    the cataphatic facet of Christian spirituality and, 65–66
    the evangelical tradition and, 72
    lectio divina and, 93–94
Boersma, Hans, on *lectio divina*, 94
boundaries, lack of between work and family. *See* boundary ambiguity
boundary ambiguity (BA), 5–6, 46–48
boundary keeping, 87–88
boundary violations, 109–10
breathing practices, 79, 85, 91–93, 101, 103
burnout. *See also* approaches to managing burnout
    acedia related to, 18

Index

burnout *(continued)*
  compassion fatigue contributing to, 16–17
  consequences of, 22–24
  Differentiation in Christ (DifC) as tool to manage, 50–58
  emotional labor contributing to, 18–20, 31–34
  formal definition and components of, 6–7, 14, 15, 16f
  manifestations of, 77
  organizational and personal mismatch contributing to, 18–20
  overview of, 13–24
  pastor self-assessment for, 105–8
  pastoral, 46–58
  research on, 7–8, 13–14, 48–49
  work-family balance (WFB) and, 18–20

cataphatic (word-based) facet of Christian spirituality, 65–66
Centering Prayer, 98–103
charismatic tradition, 70–71
Christ. *See also* Christlikeness; Differentiation in Christ; Jesus prayer
  in the evangelical tradition, 72
  as foundation for self-esteem, 51–52
  imitation of, 59, 62–63
  mindfulness practices and, 78–88
  saving work of, 64
  self-revelation and, 65
Christian devotion meditation (CDM), 59, 89–103
Christian identity, 3–5, 43–44, 50–53
Christian spirituality
  apophatic facet of, 63–65, 69
  aspects of traditions of, 62–68
  cataphatic facet of, 65–66

charismatic tradition of, 70–71
Christlikeness and, 62–63, 66–68
contemplative life tradition of, 68–69
evangelical tradition of, 72
holiness tradition of, 69–70
incarnational tradition of, 72–73
social justice tradition of, 71–72
worldview framework of, 61–62
Christlikeness, 62–63, 66–68
chronic experiences, prolonged, 15
church turnover, 23–24, 33
clergy, mindfulness practice and, 78
Cloud of the Unknowing, The (anonymous author), 63, 99
Coe, John, on contemplation (contemplative prayer), 64–65
community, church, 37
community, key area of organization life, 20, 111
compassion fatigue, 16–19
conflict, 38–39, 55–56
congregation. *See also* boundary ambiguity
  difficult decisions and, 35–36, 44–45
  pastor's burnout affecting, 18, 23–24
  the pastor's family and, 5–6, 36, 46–48, 52–58, 109–17
congregation and pastoral burnout self-reflection, 113
consequences, 22–24
contemplatio (contemplation), 95, 96
contemplation (contemplative prayer), 65
contemplative life tradition, 68–69
control, key area of organization life, 19–20, 111

134

Index

control, work and family balance and, 41–42
Copenhagen Burnout Inventory, 48
counseling congregants, 16
culture, organizational, 20, 23
culture worship in incarnational tradition, 73
cynicism
  as component of burnout, 6–7, 16f, 17–18
  defined, 15

Deacons (Smethurst), 60
deep acting, 6, 9, 28–30, 31–32
demands
  emotional, 22
  high, 77–78
  ministry, 36–37
  salience and, 5–6, 8–9, 55–57
  time, 37
depression, 24, 76–77, 85, 109
devotional Bible reading, 93–98
Differentiation in Christ (DifC)
  overview of, 1–5
  pastoral burnout and, 50–51
  salience dimension of, 5, 8, 55–57
  satisfaction dimension of, 4–5, 7–8, 51–53
  self-esteem and, 51–52, 54
Differentiation of Self (DoS)
  interpersonal, 44–45
  intrapersonal, 43
distance, 55–56
Dunbar, Scott, on work-family balance, 42

eating mindfully, 84
emotional exhaustion, 8, 31–33, 38, 48–49
emotional labor, 6, 22, 25, 28–34
enduring satisfaction, 7–8
enriching resources, 39
evangelical tradition, 72

example cases
  Michael, 30–31
  Pastor Brian, 3–5, 7, 8–9
  Pastor Joe, 19–20
  Pastor Mike, 60–61
  Pastor Tim, 19–22, 23–24, 42–45
  Pastor Will, 53–58
exhaustion
  acedia and, 17–18
  in burnout assessment, 48–49
  as component of burnout, 6–8, 16f
  coping with, 48–49
  defined, 15
  emotional as aspect of psychological strain, 38
  resulting from emotional labor, 31–33
expectations
  from the congregation, 5, 47–48
  employee/organization mismatch of, 19
  work-family conflict (WFC) and, 38–40

fairness, key area of organization life, 20–21, 111
faith, 61–62
family, pastor's. *See also* role conflict; work-family balance
  the congregation and, 36, 46–48, 52–58, 109–17
  support by enhancing work satisfaction, 39
  work-family conflict (WFC) and, 38–40
family of origin (FOO), 43–44
Foster, Richard J.
  on imagination, 94
  six Christian spiritual frameworks of, 68–73

Index

Francis, Leslie
   on exhaustion/depletion and high job satisfaction, 7, 10–11
   on professional efficacy, 52
   study of burnout and, 48–49
Francis Burnout Inventory, 48
Francis's Satisfaction in Ministry Scale, 49
Frederick, Thomas, on work-family balance, 42

glass house, life in a. *See* boundary ambiguity
glass house metaphor, 36
God
   Christian devotion meditation and, 90–103
   Christian mindfulness and, 78, 87–88
   differentiation in Christ and, 50–51
   disconnection from, 18
   mindful walking and, 85–86
   as purpose of pastoring, 49
   relationship to in apophatic and cataphatic approaches, 62–68
   relationship to in different spiritual frameworks, 68–73
   secondary callings and, 3

Hochschild, Arlie, 26
holiness tradition, 69–70
Holy Spirit, 64–65, 70

incarnational tradition, 72–73
indifference, 38
inefficacy
   as component of burnout, 6–7, 15, 16f
   relationship to absence of care, 18
   service professions and, 26–28
   strategies for managing, 28–30

intrapersonal Differentiation of Self (DoS), 44–45

Jesus Christ. *See* Christ
Jesus Prayer, 86, 90, 91–93
journaling, 82–83

Keating, Thomas, 98–99, 100–101
Keller, Tim, on the gospel, 50

lectio (reading), 95, 96
lectio divina, 93–98
Lee, Cameron, 36, 47

managing burnout. *See* approaches to managing burnout
Maslach Burnout Inventory (MBI), 48
Maslach's six areas of organizational life, 19–21, 110–11
meaning
   of Christ's death in the evangelical tradition, 72
   finding during the Jesus Prayer, 91–92
   finding in *lectio divina*, 94–95
   in life and mindfulness, 80–81
   making, 61–62, 68
   secondary callings and, 2–3
meaningfulness of ministry, 8, 48–49, 52
meditatio (meditation), 95, 96
mindful walking, 85–86
mindfulness approaches for managing burnout
   basic steps, 78–82
   boundary keeping, 87–88
   Christian mindfulness, 78
   eating, 84
   journaling, 82–83
   research involving, 75–78
   sleeping, 84–85
   walking, 85–86
ministry
   burnout impacts on, 17–21

Index

demands, 8–10, 36–37
Differentiation in Christ (DifC)
   providing resources for, 58
   family recruitment in, 109
   meaningfulness of, 8, 48–49, 52
   unaddressed stress in, 77
motivation, 67–68, 80

Oman, Doug, 61–62
oratio (prayer), 95, 96
organizational and personal mismatch, 18–20
organizational life, 18–22. *See also* Maslach's six areas of organizational life
organizational perspective, 22–24
over functioning/under functioning reciprocity, 55–56

pastoral burnout, 46–58
pastors
   acedia and, 17–18
   boundary ambiguity (BA), boundary violations and, 5–6, 46–48, 87–88, 109–10
   Christian devotion meditation (CDM) and, 11, 74, 89–90
   compassion fatigue and, 16–17
   concern over using Christian devotion meditation (CDM), 11
   consequences of burnout for, 22–24
   Differentiation in Christ for managing burnout and, 50–58
   distinction between primary and secondary callings and, 3–5
   emotional exhaustion vs. job satisfaction of, 7–9
   emotional labor of, 6, 25–28, 31–34
   emotional labor strategies of, 10, 28–31

   Francis study on pastoral burnout, 48–49
   mindfulness practices and, 75–78
   spiritual emptiness and, 11–12
   their families and, 35–45, 109–10
plan development for managing burnout
   congregation and pastoral burnout self-reflection, 113
   developing personal burnout plan, 113–15
   personal reflection on family and congregation questions, 110
   sample template for personal burnout plan, 115–20
   self-assessment, 105–8
   self-assessment reflection questions, 108–9
prayer
   the apophatic approach and, 63
   Centering Prayer, 98–103
   Jesus prayer, 86, 91–93
   John Coe on Christian contemplative, 65
   during mindful exercise, 86
   during mindful sleep, 85
   oratio, 95, 96
   in practicing *lectio divina*, 95–98
primary calling, 2–4
psychological strain, 38
purpose. *See* meaningfulness of ministry

religion vs. spirituality, 61–62
resources, enriching, 39
response vs. reaction, 81–82
reward, key area of organization life, 20, 111, 112
role conflict, 37–38

salience, 5, 8, 55–57

Index

satisfaction. *See also* meaningfulness of ministry
  as component of Differentiation in Christ (DifC), 4–5, 7–8, 43–45, 51–55
  decreased congregant, 24
  despite burnout, 17
  familial support enhancing, 39
  mindfulness and, 77–78
  work-family balance and, 40–43
  work-family conflict and, 109
Satisfaction of Ministry Scale, 49
Scripture, 67–68, 93–96
secondary callings, 2–4
self-assessment, 105–8, 113
self-assessment reflection questions, 108–9, 116–20
self-efficacy, lowered, 52
self-esteem, 51–52, 54
service professions, 26–28
sleep, 84–85
Smethurst, Matt, 60
social justice tradition, 71
spiritual practices for managing burnout
  Centering Prayer, 98–102
  Christian devotion meditation (CDM), 89–103
  Jesus Prayer, 91–93
stigma, 33
strategies for managing burnout. *See* approaches to managing burnout
stress
  causing burnout, 32
  chronic, 14–15
  efficacy of mindfulness for coping with, 75–76
  emotional processes for management of in families, 55–56
  high burnout jobs and, 33
  the Jesus prayer and, 93
  physical exercise and, 85–86
  prolonged vs. short term, 7, 14–15
  sleep and, 84–85
  unaddressed in ministry, 77
  unique to pastoral work, 3, 35–36, 46–48
stress management, four emotional processes for, 55–56
stressful experiences, prolonged, 14–15
stressors, defined, 15
suicidal ideation, 77
surface acting, 6, 9, 28–31, 32

Talbot, John, on the Jesus prayer, 91
telos (goal), 71–72
time demands, 37
traditions, aspects of Christian spiritual, 62–68
Trammel, Regina, on eating mindfully, 84
Trent, John, on eating mindfully, 84
triangulation, 55–56
turnover, 23–24, 33

values, key area of organization life, 21, 111

walking, mindful, 85–86
Whitney, Donald, on cataphatic types of spiritual disciplines, 65–66
work-family balance (WFB)
  definitions of, 39–42
  description of relationships and, 41*t*
  differentiation and, 44*f*
  emotional labor and, 21–24
  family systems and, 43–45
  overview of, 35–36
  types of relationships impacting, 38–43

Index

work and family domains, 37–38
work-family conflict (WFC), 10, 37–40, 52, 104, 109–10

workload, key area of organization life, 19, 111, 113. *See also* demands

www.ingramcontent.com/pod-product-compliance
Lightning Source LLC
Chambersburg PA
CBHW031500160426
43195CB00010BB/1049